WONDER VERSE

Dreamy Delights

First published in Great Britain in 2025 by:

Young Writers
Remus House
Coltsfoot Drive
Peterborough
PE2 9BF
Telephone: 01733 890066
Website: www.youngwriters.co.uk

FOREWORD

WELCOME READER,

For Young Writers' latest competition *Wonderverse*, we asked primary school pupils to explore their creativity and write a poem on any topic that inspired them. They rose to the challenge magnificently with some going even further and writing stories too! The result is this fantastic collection of writing in a variety of styles.

Here at Young Writers our aim is to encourage creativity in children and to inspire a love of the written word, so it's great to get such an amazing response, with some absolutely fantastic pieces. This open theme of this competition allowed them to write freely about something they are interested in, which we know helps to engage kids and get them writing. Within these pages you'll find a variety of topics, from hopes, fears and dreams, to favourite things and worlds of imagination. The result is a collection of brilliant writing that showcases the creativity and writing ability of the next generation.

I'd like to congratulate all the young writers in this anthology, I hope this inspires them to continue with their creative writing.

CONTENTS

Corby Old Village Primary School, Corby

Poppy Stephen (11)	57
Elsie Chong (9)	58
Maksymilian Olejniczak (10)	59
Eva-May Rawson (10)	60
Hollie Hearsum (10)	61
Esmee Skillern (9)	62
Chase Rankin (9)	63
Emily Hirtsch (9)	64
Amelia Grant-Coker (10)	65

Hipswell Church Of England Primary School, Hipswell

Holly Northrop (10)	66
Tayla Crofts (11)	67
Kaelynn Verah (10)	68
Sophia Fyfe (10)	69
Freya Collier (11)	70

Hoe Bridge School, Woking

Grace Beere (11)	71
Zoya Topalova Ward (9)	72
Freya Hardman (9)	76
Annika Sharma (9)	79
Gregory Avent (11)	80
Arthur Ramsey (10)	82
Daniel Whittaker (11)	84
Eleni Kavakiotis (11)	86
Vahin Akkari (10)	88
Shivanjali Kanwar Narban (11)	90
Clemmie Lees (9)	92
Freddy Aldridge (11)	94
Arjan Jutla (11)	96
Emilia Reynolds (11)	98
Matthew Janson (10)	100
Amelie Flude (10)	101
Shraddha Varambally (7)	102
Henry Damen-Turner (8)	103
Harriet Hellings (9)	104
Alya Kumar (9)	106

Avinesh Ramanathan (9)	107
Sebastian Woodall (10)	108
Wilfred Gagen (7)	109
Maisie Reid (9)	110
Edward Barrett (11)	111
Nate Ferrier (11)	112
Menaal Reza (8)	113
Harry Green (10)	114

Lower Halstow School, Lower Halstow

Josiah Orji (11)	115
Arthur Dowdell (11)	116
Cleo Cairns (11)	118
Edward Jessey (11)	120
Evie Nije (10)	121
Henry Williams (10)	122
Kian Godden (10)	124
Lara Pina (11)	125
Josephine Shilling (10)	126

Lycée International de Londres Winston Churchill, Wembley

The Magenta Class	127
Yazid Choulli (8)	128
Marlie Germain (7)	130
Marina Baldini (8)	131
Chloé Shahbahrami	132
Isabella Laborieux (7)	133
Georgia Le Junter-Sleath (8)	134
Kaimu Brugger (8)	135
Ava Daniel (8)	136
Venkat Sundaram Lee (9)	137
Zoé Adjido (7)	138
Aline Bachir (7)	139
Neil Gala (7)	140
Noah Lepelletier (7)	141
Jasper Josias (7)	142

Marshwood CE Primary School, Marshwood

Archie Winnett (11)	143
Tabby Travill (9)	144
Rosie Knight (8)	145
Kiki Crane (10)	146
Grace Johnson (8)	147
Louisa Grinter (9)	148
Edith Hooper (10)	149
Ivy Partridge (7)	150
Humphrey Leeds (8)	151
Erin Churchill (10)	152
Elsie Ballam (11)	153
Charlie Battershell (9)	154
Albert Brum (7)	155

Pinewood School, Bourton

Bea Godfree (10)	156
Wilf Llewellyn (10)	158
Arlo Dawson	160
Roxie Spooner	162
Guy Ashcroft (9)	163
Ivo Eddell (9)	164
William Newham (9)	166
Augusto Aquitania (9)	167
Louis Leach (9)	168
Amelia Goodhew (9)	170
Davina Woolley (9)	172
Alistair Wilson (10)	174
Maya Lewis (10)	175
Elise Campbell (11)	176
Monty Dearden (10)	177
Xander Clarke (10)	178
Dhruv Chukka (10)	179
Esme Erskine Crum (10)	180
Sebastian Dobney (9)	181
William Mackay (11)	182
Francesca Walker (10)	183
Mary Ingham (10)	184
Arthur Ferguson (11)	185
Archie Colquhoun (11)	186
Max Heaton (10)	187

Max Tilney (10)	188
Rosie Lawless (11)	189
Florrie Horton (9)	190
Imogen Workman (11)	191
Lily Lewis (10)	192
Joe Rajapaksha	193
Freddie Campbell (11)	194
Reggie Parsons (11)	195
Martha Hyde-Smith (11)	196
Ruan Moelwyn-Hughes (11)	197
George Wynn-Williams (9)	198
Valentina Kidson-Trigg (10)	199
James Hosken	200
Bella Russell (10)	201
Annie Sharman (10)	202
Beattie Simons (9)	203
Aluna Angus (10)	204
Rose Bartlam (9)	205
Theia Grewal (9)	206
Petra Durrant (9)	207
Alice Longe (10)	208
Archie Giverin (11)	209
Wilfrid Bird (11)	210
Georgia Finch	211
Fenner Owen (11)	212
Quintus Vero (10)	213
Arthur Clark (10)	214
Harry John (9)	215
Jack Woddy (9)	216
Alex Tomanek (11)	217
Freddie Leggate (10)	218
Julius Steele (11)	219
Oscar Subba (11)	220
Rory	221
Ben Workman (9)	222
Ivo Robertson (10)	223
Adam Willis-Hill (11)	224
Harry Vane-Tempest (11)	225
Charlie Gantlett (9)	226
Max Charlton (10)	227
Duncan Ogilvy (10)	228
Jack Moss (10)	229
Issy Lloyd (10)	230

Pix Brook Academy, Arlesey

Tate Osborn (9)	231
Rex Osborn (11)	232
Ewan Ronayne (11)	233
Florence Harris (9)	234
Eden Chegwyn-Ross (9)	235
Tyler Jones (11)	236

Rose Lane Primary School, Romford

Louisa Short (10)	237
Noah Jolaoso (9)	238
Abdullah Ahmed (10)	240

Roseacres Primary School, Takeley

Jessica Waring (9)	241
Lacey Fuller (8)	242
Sophia Taylor (9)	243
Jaxon Larman (8)	244
Ella Felton (8)	245
Thyri Cherrill (8)	246

St Mary Magdalene And St Stephen's CE Primary School, London

Khadija Bashir (7)	247
Hamza Tabesh (7)	248

St Timothy's Primary RC School, Glasgow

Kyle Fleming (11)	249
Jay Barwell (11)	250
Radiant Lombardo (11)	251
Hana Zebri (10)	252
Aarron Maley Turnbull (12)	253

Weddington Primary School, Nuneaton

Evie Fallon (9)	254
Kenayah Kisempia (9)	255
Amelie Thomas (8)	256
Theo Wright (8)	257
Scarlett Pearce (8)	258
Seth Thomas (9)	259
Olly King (8)	260
Edward Swift (9)	261
Jacob Wright (9)	262
Oliwia Swietoslawska (9)	263
Chloe Ivers (8)	264
Clayton Lai (9)	265

West Wimbledon Primary School, Raynes Park

Bonnie Withers (10)	266
Shezmin Shameer (9)	267
Patrik Moise (10)	268
Madeline Moorfield (9)	269

THE POEMS AND STORIES

Super Space

Zooming around the universe.
What planets have been cursed?
What might go beyond our sight?
Maybe it's a burning light.
What magic have you got?
Maybe you could, or maybe not.
Is there an end to endless space?
And does everything have a face?
How many secrets can there be?
Not many that we can see.
Twinkle, twinkle, little star.
Can you go super far?
Can I exit the Milky Way?
Will it take seven days?
When will the Earth be gone?
Then there's nothing that can be done.
Will I ever get out there?
You, I dare!
With me, I'd be floating around.
With nothing making a sound.

Leon Moore (9)
Bengeo Primary School, Bengeo

The Mysterious Forest

Branches are jagged.
Fog shrouds the place.
A veil of mystery cloaks the wood.
Secrets are waiting to be found.
No one would dare to venture here.
All you would see are dull colours.
The loneliness makes a strange atmosphere in the forest,
It is almost as if it's stuck in dusk.
Mysteriousness lurks within,
It creates a treacherous land.
What lives beyond is unknown,
One step into the forest would barricade you in thorns.
Only a glimpse of the forest can be seen with the naked eye.
Dark flora paints the place
The forest creates a landscape full of wonder.

Nathaniel Morgans (10)
Bengeo Primary School, Bengeo

Save The Sea Otters

I'm swimming in the sea
Leaping joyfully
Please now let me be
I'm swimming in the sea

I'm munching on fish
A special big wish
I'm giving my tail a big swish
I'm munching on fish

I'm in danger
So we're all in danger
Things are just getting stranger
I'm in danger

I'm getting scanned
I've been brought onto land
Lend a helping hand
I'm getting scanned

I'm swimming in the sea
Leaping joyfully
Please now let me be
To be finally free!

Alya Gocoldas (8)
Bengeo Primary School, Bengeo

When The Sun Sets

When the sun sets,
The magic will rise.
All light arrives,
Seeing things you've never seen.
Growing a big fat bean,
Seeing butterflies,
Making bread,
Growing a tree,
In the middle of a bag,
Everything is possible,
In the world of magic.
Seeing new things,
Making a tree house,
Having a hummingbird as a pet,
No one ever dies,
Seeing seagulls race by,
As the wind blows the trees.
Rainbows hiding in an ever-dark corner,
Shellfish hiding in the sand.
There's nothing like Magic Land.

Elowen Sullivan
Bengeo Primary School, Bengeo

Winter

Winter is here
The season has begun
Gentle snow is drifting
And the village bells have rung

Everyone is inside
Close up and warm by the fire
Sipping their hot cocoa
As piles of snow start to get higher

People outside
Playing and having fun
Children having snowball fights
As other children run

Winter is fun
But it won't last forever
Spring will come soon
So make sure your snowmen aren't in the warm
weather.

Jaanu Bandy (9)
Bengeo Primary School, Bengeo

Anglo-Saxons

My hands are chopped off if I steal a pig
I'm never ever bored, there's always a job
The punishments in my days are always so gruesome
I worship Woden and Thunor as my gods
Most of us live in a part of the Heptarchy
My mum's away, my dad's a metal forger
The jumper I am wearing is made from nettles
Anglo-Saxon times are the best times for me.

Elena Fignon (9)
Bengeo Primary School, Bengeo

Kittens

K ittens are intrigued by the world.

I thought that kittens were scared of it.

T he kittens always have a mind of their own.

T he adult cats protect their babies at all times.

E very species of cat and kitten has a personality of their own.

N ot every cat and kitten gets a home.

S ome cats and kittens could be yours!

Sophia Benedetti (8)
Bengeo Primary School, Bengeo

What Are Space's Secrets?

Zooming around the universe,
What planets have been cursed?
Is there magic there or not?
What secrets have you got?
Sizzling, secretive, sinister space,
How many planets have a face?
Supersonic shooting stars,
As bright as magical Mars,
What could be beyond our sight?
Maybe it is a burning light?

Riley Cable (9)
Bengeo Primary School, Bengeo

Endangered Animals

Save these animals
With their soft but bumpy shells

Save these animals
Gracefully gliding through the ocean

Save these animals
With their smooth skin that glimmers like emeralds

Save these animals
They give birth to babies in the sand

Can you guess what it is?
A turtle.

Sophie Eddleston (9)
Bengeo Primary School, Bengeo

Unicorn Magic

Flying through the sky
As they say goodbye
Twinkling in the night
What a wonderful sight
Moving their hooves
To the groove
Putting a smile on people's faces
As they leave their magical traces.

Maira Usman (11)
Bolton Parish Church CE Primary School, Bolton

The Lionesses Are Loud And Proud

The Lionesses play with heart
Each and every game they start
Mary Earps makes a brilliant save
Diving for the ball, she is so brave
Lucy Bronze defends with all her might
She keeps the team steady, day and night
Millie Bright plays with such grace
Her tackles are quick, she sets the pace
Keira Walsh controls the midfield with ease
Her passes are smooth, like a summer breeze
Lauren Hemp weaves through, so quick and smart
Her skills and visions are works of art
Chloe Kelly joins the fight
Her skills and passion shine so bright
Alessia Russo takes charge of the ball
She's the greatest of them all
Sarina Wiegman leads the team
It's so nice to see her beam
One day, I will play there too
Dreaming big and seeing it through.

Matilda Hibbs (9)
Bourton-On-The-Water Primary School, Bourton On The Water

Creatures

As you go to sleep at dusk, a little winged human is
waking, ready to roam the night
(She could never have a fright).
An abandoned golf cart? No.
A fairy playground? Yes...
"But who do I play with? Nobody here.
Ooh, what's that? Wait, I haven't seen them around.
Maybe it speaks bird.
It looks like a lovebird.
Yes! Wait, it has butterfly wings.
Finally, a friend. First, I ask for its name, Butterlove.
What gender? Girl. How old? Ten. Favourite food?
Pizza.
Cool, me too!"
And the two play for the rest of the night!

Violet Ronald (9)
Bourton-On-The-Water Primary School, Bourton On The Water

The Lionesses!

T oday, Lionesses still stand tall.

H annah Hampton ready to rumble.

E sme Morgan moving to Washington Spirit.

L eah Williamson leader of them all,

"I am always ready," says loving, lively Lorna!

O f course they score the best goal

N ever are they tired or moody.

E lla Toone standing up for Alessia Russo.

S aving made it all amazing!

S omebody made their debut,

E llie Roebuck stopping all balls.

S tanway attacking all the opposition.

Elsie Lunnon-Wood (9)
Bourton-On-The-Water Primary School, Bourton On The Water

Chocolate Spread

All chocolate is delicious, from milk to dark and white,
But don't forget about Nutella, it really is a delight.
I spread it thick upon my bread, my toast, my
pancakes, too,
It's a sticky brown delight I like to call chocolate glue.
It sticks my strawberries, blueberries and banana to my
pancake,
And adds an extra flavour to any fantastic milkshake.
I really love this chocolate spread,
Its nutty taste just fills my head
With thoughts of what I can do.
With Nutella, it's a dream food come true.

Nancy Hoffman (9)
Bourton-On-The-Water Primary School, Bourton On The Water

Walk Like An Egyptian

Over Africa, the sun shone down on Egypt,
On the dry desert below, Tutankhamun skipped.
Tutankhamun loved statues and gold,
He wanted them all before he got old.
He used slaves to build big pointy towers,
They were called pyramids, they took hours and hours
and hours!
Egypt's length is 880 miles.
It has the world's longest river, and it's called the Nile.
When kings and queens died, they were buried in a
tomb,
Surrounded by hieroglyphs and gold in a locked-away
room.

Darcie Broomfield (8)
Bourton-On-The-Water Primary School, Bourton On The Water

Redemption Song

Dead at thirty-six
A legend in life and beyond
Someone once tried to shoot him
But for them, it went horribly wrong
His music brings feelings of love and harmony
The soulful sounds of reggae
'Get Up, Stand Up' and 'Redemption Song'
People still listen across the world today

His motto was to spread peace, not war
He sold out arenas and went on tour
This year, he would have been eighty
The greatest of all time, Bob Marley!

Reginald O'Toole (7)
Bourton-On-The-Water Primary School, Bourton On The Water

Space And Planets

S pace is sparse,
P lanets like Mars,
A black hole lies unpassed,
C omets zooming fast,
E legant astronauts floating in space!

And

P lanets are big and small,
L ike a colourful ball,
A beautiful ring is on some planets,
N othing shines like our sun's light,
E very star shines bright,
T oo many stars, not any more,
S o much more we need to explore!

Emil Romanowski (9)
Bourton-On-The-Water Primary School, Bourton On The Water

Egyptians

E thnic group of people from the Nile River Valley.

G etting together to celebrate the deaths of innocent people.

Y ears went past, civilisation vanished.

P yramids are the symbol of its greatness.

T he city of Cairo buzzing with life.

I ntimidating ships squeezing through the Suez Canal.

A frica's gate to the world.

N ile River full of beauty and danger.

S phinx towering over the desert.

Jakub Kadziolka (9)
Bourton-On-The-Water Primary School, Bourton On The Water

Universe

U nique planets are all around us

N eptune is freezing, and to live there would be too dangerous

I n our solar system, the sun is powerful and massive

V enus has clouds that are filled with acid

E ven Mars is impressive with the biggest mountain of all

R ings of Saturn, made of dust and rocks, look super cool

S cary black holes could suck everything in

E arth is our planet, and it's just amazing.

Jake Harfield (8)
Bourton-On-The-Water Primary School, Bourton On The Water

Cosmic Conga

If you look up in the sky tonight,
You will see an amazing sight.
The planets will all be in a line,
And visible from your place and mine.

Saturn's rings will look like a star,
Beautiful even from afar.
On either side of the moon.
Better get your binoculars soon!

So, I think it is definitely worth,
Seeing this amazing scene from Earth.
With Neptune, Jupiter and Mars.
A spectacular parade in the stars!

Myles Mukherji (9)
Bourton-On-The-Water Primary School, Bourton On The Water

Volcanoes

Rumble, rumble
Grumble, grumble
Boom!
Black smoke covers the sky
Lava flows as people run in terror
Black smoke fills the air as the volcano
Spews out lava as fast as a cheetah
The lava grows
Rumble, rumble
Grumble, grumble
Silence.

Femke Van Dijk (9)
Bourton-On-The-Water Primary School, Bourton On The Water

All About The Red Pandas

R ed and white tails
E ating bamboo non-stop
D reaming throughout the day

P laying with its furry pals
A bout in the trees so high
N ot afraid and always happy
D ozing in the summer sun
A s night draws in they say goodnight.

Millie J (9)
Bourton-On-The-Water Primary School, Bourton On The Water

Friendship

Friends are helpful but not mean
Friends are truthful and don't lie
And here is some more poetry for you
Friends are sorry, but not in *the stop-doing kind of way*
Friends play with you
Then friends help you
Not leave you there.

Wandile Mangena (8)
Bourton-On-The-Water Primary School, Bourton On The Water

Colours Of Nature

Yellow is a bitter lemon
Blue is a fat blueberry
Pink is a fuzzy peach
Red is a sharp rose
Purple is a unique lavender
Brown is a spiky pine cone
My personal favourite is...
An orange orange!

Clara Wingrove (7)
Bourton-On-The-Water Primary School, Bourton On The Water

Oh Egypt

Oh Egypt, gift of the Nile.
Where cats are worshipped as gods,
Where pyramids, mummies, and tombs remain,
A gateway to the past,
Where Isis and Osiris speak in whispers.

Bella-Mae Masardo (7)
Bourton-On-The-Water Primary School, Bourton On The Water

Friendship

Friends are kind, not mean.
And they play with you basically every day.
They are funny and make you laugh.
If you're sad, they can turn your frown into a smile.

Amelia Uzzell (8)
Bourton-On-The-Water Primary School, Bourton On The Water

My Cats

Coco and Muffin, a mischievous pair,
Dashing around without a care.
Coco, fluffy with colours so bright,
Muffin, sleek in her black-orange light.

Greedy for treats they both demand,
Muffin meows with an impatient sound,
Coco just waits, a cunning glance,
Then pounces on laces when given the chance.

Toy mice scatter as they chase and play,
Zooming through rooms in a frantic display,
Under the table, over the chair,
No quiet moment, not one to spare!

Muffin will yowl when dinner is late,
Coco just sits and accepts her fate.
But when the bowl finally comes in sight,
Both dive in with pure delight.

Jessica Whittaker (8)
Bricknell Primary School, Hull

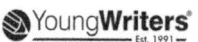
The Blasting Seasons Of Nature

The year kicks off with January,
Winter means no leaves on trees,
Then we get to February,
Where trees still have no leaves,
By the time we get to March,
The leaves are growing back,
Halfway through spring is April,
It is time for chocolatey snacks,
With Easter just gone, it's May,
Warmer weather is here, yay,
It's time to get out and play,
Summer is well on the way,
Temperatures are rising again,
But there is still rain in June,
This is really good for nature,
All the flowers will have bloomed,
July and August are holiday seasons,
Let's all go to the beach,
There are six weeks off for kids,
So teachers don't need to teach.
Back to school in September,

A new season is calling,
Here, we call it autumn,
That's when leaves start falling,
One of the funnest months of the year,
October, there's Halloween,
Trick or treat to all out there,
How many ghosts have you seen?
After the fun, it's November,
Again, winter is on the way,
Christmas soon means Santa's watching,
So you better behave,
The year ends with December,
It's like Christmas every day,
We are all filled with excitement,
Families and friends can't wait,
That's twelve months of the year,
365 days,
All the four seasons,
Are special in their own ways.

Ava Lane (9)
Bricknell Primary School, Hull

Nature Is A Wonderful Thing

The fairies were flying all around,
Around the flowers, up and down,
The trees were swaying left and right,
But no more fairies left in sight.

The sun came out, birds were singing,
The children at school could hear the bells ringing.
Children were planting seeds in a pot,
But it was very hot.

The month went so fast,
The children saw their flowers grow at last,
The smiling faces made a teacher sing,
Isn't nature a wonderful thing?

Maddie Caisley (9)
Bricknell Primary School, Hull

Winter

Winter, crisp, cold as the North Pole.
Winter, snow everywhere while children play.
Winter, Christmas cheer in the aromatic air.
Winter, gifts galore from Christmas.
Winter, radiators on in every single home.
Winter, houses in a mess from the enchanting elves.
Winter, fairs and happy people.
Winter, time for being jolly.
Winter, free time with family.
Winter, fun as a resort.
Winter is very fun and we should appreciate it.

Arhaan Zaman (9)
Bricknell Primary School, Hull

The Little Cute Bunny

Once upon a time, there was a bunny called Bella. Bella went to school but she got bullied. Her mum did not like it.

She asked, "Do you want to get bullied? Bunny honey?"

"No."

"Do you want to go to school?"

"Yes."

"Okay, you can go to school."

She got bullied again.

Her mum said to the boy, "Stop it now!" and the boy stopped bullying Bella.

Lena Rahman (9)

Bricknell Primary School, Hull

Sid The Snake

I was surprised one day,
When I was skipping on my way,
To grab myself a delicious milkshake,
When I bumped into a slithering snake.
He was bright green,
And could be easily seen,
While he was chilling on a bench,
Reading his magazine.
I approached the snake,
He said his name was Sid.
As he slid over to me
And I bolted with a scream,
As I didn't want to be seen!

Ella Grainger (9)
Bricknell Primary School, Hull

Some Foxes...

Some foxes are shy and like to hide in boxes.
Some foxes frolic freely like the wind, whilst they also
raid things that have been binned.
Some foxes are silver, some are red, surprisingly, none
of them sleep in a bed.
Some foxes are kind, although they find us scary.
Some foxes like to run on their legs to go and eat some
eggs.
I know a fox that lives in a box, but that box is where I
keep my socks.

Olive Appleyard (9)
Bricknell Primary School, Hull

Forever Friendships

Break up, make up, do each other's make-up,
Best friends, best friends,
Never leave each other,
Acting like we're brother and brother.

Best friends, best friends,
Always stick together,
No matter if it's colder or warmer weather.

Best friends, best friends,
Are by each other's side,
No matter if we drop through the wind,
Or we glide.

Seth Joplin (9)
Bricknell Primary School, Hull

Nature Plants/Flower Addiction

I had a flower stuck in a tower
It had a stain but it started to rain.

There were flowers with some healing powers.
I cannot wait for spring because flowers are my thing.

I love flowers from the petal to the stem.
Tulips, roses, lavender, all of them!

I can spend many hours
Watering my flowers.

In my garden I go
To watch my flowers grow.

Ava Regan (9)
Bricknell Primary School, Hull

Hidden Heroes

Superheroes are super cool,
And they beat the bad guys when they try to rule.
They have to train all day
They never come out to play.
They have super strength
They can stretch to any length
They've got supervision
To see any collision
But parents were the heroes all along
When we are near them, they make us feel super strong.

Archer Lowsley (8)
Bricknell Primary School, Hull

The Ocean

The big blue ocean where fish swim
And the whale sings out its glorious hymn

Starfish cling to rocks below
The tide sweeps by its ebb and flow
On the seabed floor, a shipwreck, rest in peace
While life is abundant on the coral reef
We need to save our oceans, make them clean
Stop plastic pollution, we must go green.

Frankie Baird (9)
Bricknell Primary School, Hull

The Fastest Animal Around

Cheetahs are the fastest animal around,
Anyone faster can't be found,
Unless they are running for more than a minute,
Then their prey will get away with it!
They camouflage cheekily with their spots.
They're covered in them, lots and lots.
Cheetahs are my favourite cat,
But maybe don't give them a pat.

Hazel Brant (9)
Bricknell Primary School, Hull

The Four Seasons

Beautiful sunflowers starting to bloom.
Lighting up the whole room.

The sun shining high and bright.
Feeling its warmth is such a delight.

The leaves are falling off, what a sight.
Now to prepare for my conker fight.

The crunchy snow under my feet.
Makes me lose all the heat.

Emily Bunn (8)
Bricknell Primary School, Hull

Seasons

It is sunny in the summer and rainy in the winter
Spring is the best and autumn is the worst
Flowers grow and grass grows
But sometimes it grows very slow
Spring is green and autumn is Halloween
That is all for the seasons today
Maybe next time I could do it again.

Heba Alazzam (8)
Bricknell Primary School, Hull

Summer

Blossoms grow on trees
Leaves sparkle with green
The sun warms up
Keeping us warm
Chicks walking around with their eggs
Holding pegs
The air is hot
Plants growing in pots
When I look out my window
I see people playing limbo
Summer is amazing.

Lakshya Kathirkamlingam (8)
Bricknell Primary School, Hull

Vegetables

I love eating vegetables
Vegetables are my favourite

I eat them all the time
As they taste so fine

They are very very healthy
They are good for your heart

But the only trouble is
That they make you...

Fart!

Poppy Mould (8)
Bricknell Primary School, Hull

The Vicious Snake And Seasons

Inside the snake's house, a sparkling diamond up high,
A flower is kept near his bed, looking up to the sky.

Summer is shining so softly, the birds are singing,
Autumn is looming, and winter is waving,
Spring sets the season for new beginnings.

Emilia Allen (8)
Bricknell Primary School, Hull

Space

S aturn, a planet in our solar system.

P hysics, the study of objects in our universe.

A stronaut, a human who works in space such as Neil Armstrong.

C omets, icy bodies that orbit the sun.

E arth, the only planet with H2O.

Phyllis NG (8)

Bricknell Primary School, Hull

Spring Is Here!

Bunny tails are bobbing
Snowdrops are blooming
Blossoms are budding
Daffodils are shining
Foxes are hiding
Candyfloss skies
Tippity-tap, raindrops splat
Nights are getting shorter
Spring is here!

Ada Ostara Witts (8)
Bricknell Primary School, Hull

I Don't Like Limes

I don't like limes
My dad likes limes
This poem rhymes
I've wasted my time
I'm eating limes
In my own time
I used it to make this poem rhyme
I don't know why
I'm still eating limes.

Elham Mohammadi (9)
Bricknell Primary School, Hull

The World Of Emotions

When I got out of bed,
I was sad,
I was mad,
I was glad,
This is the world of emotions,
And I have a promotion,
And I started a commotion,
And I put on some lotion,
And I made a potion.

Muna Oleka (8)
Bricknell Primary School, Hull

Space

S un is a planet.

P lanets have solar systems.

A s Earth spins around the sun, places get hotter.

C alypso is the moon of Saturn.

E arth is our home.

Daisy Blakey (8)
Bricknell Primary School, Hull

Not-Normal Nature

A fox in a box,
A deer with big fears,
Flowers with powers,
That is crazy,
This is not normal nature,
Lots of animals here and there,
All having fun together.

Setarah Rizzoee (8)
Bricknell Primary School, Hull

Pumpkin

A haiku

Perfect pumpkins grow
Yummy pumpkins, spice lattes
Orange, green and white.

Scarlett-Leigh Hulme (9)
Bricknell Primary School, Hull

Coloured Emotions

A haiku

Yellow is happy
Orange is anxiety
Seeing red as rage.

Seb Burnell (9)
Bricknell Primary School, Hull

Hard Life

A haiku

Little grass sprouting
Luckily it finds ways well
It lives on and on.

Zachary Cook (8)
Bricknell Primary School, Hull

Sweet Pop!

Icky, sticky bubblegum
Blow! Blow! Pop!
Just a walk to the shop
And you've got yourself a pop!
For less than a pound
You don't need much wealth

A soft and chewy delight
Sounds just right
A sugary cloud
That swirls in your mouth
Nothing can go south

Can be a sticky mess
No need to stress
With a flavour so sweet
It makes you think
You could eat it all day
And never drift away

Joy in every bite
Colours are so bright
What a perfect treat
Playful and stretchy

Blow a big bubble
And watch it pop!

Eden Omadeli (10)
Cardwell Primary School, Woolwich

Nature

A lovely fragrance dances upon the air,
The sweet and gentle rose in full bloom is there,
Delicate petals dance with colourful pearls,
Yellow and pink, orange and white,
Brings colour to the garden, a radiant sight,

The lily stands tall and elegant,
With petals so pure it makes us all stare.

Claire Idehen (11)
Cardwell Primary School, Woolwich

Mental Heath Matters

M indfulness
E mbrace your feelings
N ever disrespect other people
T ake care of family and friends
A lways be kind to others
L ittle things matter.

H elping others takes nothing but love
E at healthily
A lways socialise
L ittle things can hurt
T ake responsibility
H ave respect.

M ental health matters
A lways treat people the way you want to be treated
T ry your best
T alk about your feelings
E njoy life
R ealise what you say before saying it
S tay safe.

Poppy Stephen (11)
Corby Old Village Primary School, Corby

Bubble Land

B ubbles pop,

U guys will be speechless when you walk in,

B ubbles pop! When you touch them,

B ubbles shine bright in the light,

L and of all land is magical,

E nter the magical land of bubbles!

L etters and clues all around to see if you can find the sweetie parlour,

A lso, a bubble theatre which is filled with bubbles,

N o one is allowed to go in the keep-out room, could be bubbles all around you,

D on't you wish you could be here? It will be the time of your life.

Elsie Chong (9)
Corby Old Village Primary School, Corby

Tha Magnificent Mythical Creatures

Into the land where everything is planned,
Where devils trip on pebbles.
Where dragons play bat using wagons,
Unicorns eat a ton of corn.
Where leprechauns say, "Hi, prawn,"
And Minotaurs play guitars.
The phoenixes get help from medics,
And griffins stiffen.
Where cerberuses are very cultural,
The centaurs go to the shopping centre.
Mermaids eat lots of Marmite,
Where krakens make a large racket.

Maksymilian Olejniczak (10)
Corby Old Village Primary School, Corby

Mental Health

Making people confident about their looks
Entertaining other people when they need it
Not bullying others
Treating others how you want to be treated
All people are different
Let people be themselves
Helping others
Eating is normal
A bully making you hurt yourself is not okay
Listen to people when they need someone to listen
Telling your feelings is okay.

Eva-May Rawson (10)
Corby Old Village Primary School, Corby

A Dog Called Jeff

A dog named Jeff,
Is half blind, half deaf
But people love him the same
And that makes him very tame.
He loves his bone,
He chews it at home,
He is the best of good boys,
So they give him lots of toys,
He chases his tail,
It gives people a wail,
Of excitement of course,
Because he is as big as a horse.

Hollie Hearsum (10)
Corby Old Village Primary School, Corby

Flowers

F lowers gleaming in the distance,

L ovely, live, living, sweet,

O range, red, pink, blue flowers sleeping in the bush,

W indy days wake up the flowers,

E very petal is bright and beautiful,

R ising every summer,

S lowly growing bigger and bigger.

Esmee Skillern (9)

Corby Old Village Primary School, Corby

The Acrostic Of Space

S pace is like a never-ending world,
P ortals like the Milky Way and the black hole,
A mazing as amazing can get,
C osmic world,
E nding all of space is also ending all planets.

Chase Rankin (9)
Corby Old Village Primary School, Corby

Sloth

S weet and soft,

L ovely creature,

O ften very, very slow,

T he sloth is a very fast swimmer,

H ow slow can you go?

Emily Hirtsch (9)

Corby Old Village Primary School, Corby

The Reality Of Friendship

A haiku

Beginnings and ends,
Friendship is fun but toxic,
It is about trust.

Amelia Grant-Coker (10)
Corby Old Village Primary School, Corby

Code Name: Besties

My bestie and I, like sisters we'd be,
Running through fields, wild and free.
Sometimes we'd cry, but we'd cheer up fast,
Our friendship was strong, something meant to last.
We're military kids, brave and cool,
So making new friends, that's kind of our rule.
My dad's a medic, hers an engineer,
Both serving with courage, protecting what's dear.
Then one day, I had to move away,
And my bestie went to boarding school to stay,
We didn't want to, it made us both sad,
Losing each other felt so bad.
I've met new friends, but I miss those times,
Of laughter, holding hands, and saying things in rhymes.
And while we're apart, I miss her each day,
I wish she was here, so we could always play.

Holly Northrop (10)
Hipswell Church Of England Primary School, Hipswell

The Little Flower

As I walked into my room,
I saw my little flower bloom.
I watched, in shock, as the little flower
Opened a portal in my room.

I didn't know what to do
Until the little flower said, "Doom! Doom!"
I ran to my parents' room
But it was gone, replaced with a pumpkin
That went *boom!*

I was blown back into my room
With a *bang!* And a *boom!*
I turned to the portal and soon I saw
That the little flower that had just bloomed
Had started to shine blue.

Soon, it flew out of the window
And to the moon.

Tayla Crofts (11)
Hipswell Church Of England Primary School, Hipswell

The Wretched Bear

Whose teddy bear is that?
I think I know,
Its owner is utterly sad though.
It is, in fact, a tale of woe,
I observe her frown, I cry hello.
She gives her teddy bear a shake,
And sobs until the tears make,
The only other sounds the break,
Of distant waves as the birds awake.
The bear is soft, airy and deep,
But she has a promise to keep.
Until then she cannot sleep.
She lies in her bed with ducts that weep.
She rises from her bitter bed.
With thoughts of sadness in her head.
She idolises being dead.
Facing the day,
With never-ending dread...

Kaelynn Verah (10)
Hipswell Church Of England Primary School, Hipswell

Friend Over Bully

The friends that are with you for your ups and downs,
Deserve to be with you when you get a crown.
The boys and girls who bully you,
Don't deserve to be friends with you.
Spend time with the ones you trust,
And not with the ones that will break your heart.
Believe in yourself, even if you're scared,
You always have that one friend that you know cares.
Go through life with your best friends,
And make sure that the journey never ends,
And leave the bullies behind.

Sophia Fyfe (10)
Hipswell Church Of England Primary School, Hipswell

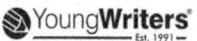

Skies Of Seasons

Light ultramarine blue skies above our heads
Turn into dark antique violet before our deceiving eyes.
We stare at the starry horizon as we fall asleep.
Under the midnight navy and royal indigo skies.
We dream in winter, wake up in summer.
Light baby blue spring skies turn into cosmic violet
As we sleep under the champagne-blush-coloured
stars.

Freya Collier (11)
Hipswell Church Of England Primary School, Hipswell

The Waltzing Willow

As the sun rises on this beautiful lawn,
Thy birdsong starts up, children arrive in joy.
It's a warm spring morning, the best time of the year,
A seed has been planted, did it take ten years?
Well, yes! I shall tell you, that's why you're here,
To hear thy great story of the willow waltzing over
there.

As time went on this great willow tree grew,
As the willow tree grew, you grew too!
It continued rising to exceeding heights,
When it reached the top, nature's delights.

This willow was the guardian of ponds, reeds galore!
It protects that alone and it protects so much more.

This willow tree finds great peace at night,
When no sound can be heard, not even some mice.

It sways all day, and it sways all night,
It performs a dance like a waltz at the pond.

So as the sun goes down on this beautiful lawn,
Thy birdsong quiets and no more is the warm.
It's a cool spring evening, the most quiet time of year,
And this is the tale of the waltzing willow, so listen and
hear.

Grace Beere (11)
Hoe Bridge School, Woking

71

Love On The Run

The sky was spears of lightning,
And the thunder was loud and frightening.
The lake was rolling around,
The wind was shaking the ground.
The rain was bullets from heaven,
And the riders were marching in sevens.

Bell wore a shirt of leather,
As she galloped through the heather.
She also bore boots of grey,
As she fed her horse some hay.
She had a ring of ruby,
As she waited for the newbies.

Over the footpath she went,
There was no sign of her tent.
She rode towards her love,
And she brought him a dove.
She wanted to make him happy,
The dove was small and flappy.

At last she arrived to him,
And she stood at the foot of the inn.
She knocked on the door with a smile,
She was weary, she'd ridden for a while.

And out of the door came a cat,
That came to her feet and then sat.

Who followed her out of the door?
'Twas her love who comes from the moor.
She greeted him with a kiss.
"So, what have I missed?"
"Football on the pitch,
And a few times raiding the rich."

"Where does that money end?"
"It ends wherever I send,
Otherwise known as the poor."
"I knew you opened a door."
They knew just what to say,
They spoke till the storm went away.

Little did Bell know,
That through the sleet and snow,
A small amount of men,
With their leader Ben,
Were marching, marching nearer.
Though some of the men there feared her.

She was known as the ghost of the town,
For when robbing, she wore a white gown
And as the men approached,

A couple of eggs were poached.
But only as the danger was near,
The danger coming was feared.

"My love, my dear, we must leave,
Yes, yes, we must weave,
Weave our way through the thicket,
Across the field of crickets."
"But why, oh why must we go
Across the thicket of low?"

"Because we are being hunted,
And because they must have confronted,
Confronted their fear of me,"
She said with a slight touch of glee.
"Well, I guess that's that then,
Oh no! I see the men!"

They got on Bell's horse in time,
And brought George's cat Lime.
George is the love of Bell,
And by then it was easy to tell.
That the men were coming in hot,
And their speed was growing a lot.

Bell, George and Lime rode far,
And then they stopped at a bar.

After they had a quick drink,
They left as quick as a blink.
They rode for hours more straight,
Until they reached a large gate.

When they entered this place,
They jolted down their pace.
They found a wedding shop,
So, they gathered lots of crops.
For this was their biggest day,
And the stage was set with some hay.

There were so little invites,
And the lights were a brilliant sight.

Then...

I do...
Me too...

"Bell, George, Bell, George, Bell, George!"

Zoya Topalova Ward (9)
Hoe Bridge School, Woking

Sleeping Beauty

Sleeping Beauty was quite dumb,
Thought she was the number one,
Got cursed for one hundred years,
Her dad cried, her mum was in tears,
Still she stayed deep in sleep,
And no one dared to take a peep.

Until one day, a handsome twit,
With jewels and stuff and quite a bit,
He vowed he would brave
The thorny bushes just to save,
The stupid, arrogant, petty princess,
Then, to marry her to his success.

But the other princes came,
All like the first one, totally insane,
Then a stupid prince tried to hack
With his sword, which he'd pack,
Everywhere he went,
But still the impenetrable thorns sent,
Him back home,
With a very angry tone.

And then, ever since,
Sent home was every prince.

All except one,
And he declared that it was done,

"I am the one who will brave,
These horrid old thorns to save,
Sleeping Beauty whom I crave!"

He hacked and hacked - with his sword,
Towards,
A massive castle with a tower,
And he stood there for an hour.
Finally, he climbed up the tower
(It took him half an hour)
With his terribly small amount of power.

When he got to the top, he didn't dare,
To peek at who lay there.
He simply just took their hand,
But he didn't dare to stand,
So, kneeling down on one knee,
He kissed the thing, but oh dear, let's see,
The girl was a good-looking troll - his face wasn't
pretty!
He'd ventured into the Land of Troll,
Oh, the poor fool's soul!
The angry troll shrieked about,
And then began to shout!

"Hey, you ain't my kind,
Look and I think you'll find,
So now your bones I shall grind!"

Then, she wrestled him to the bed,
And then he was dead!

But the stable boy who, ever since,
Had felt sorry for the poor prince,
Poisoned the troll's tea!
Well, let's see...

At first, she began to shout,
All about,

"Oh, my,
Oh, goodbye!"
She said,
And then she dropped dead!
Well, that's how I spun,
Sleeping Beauty and now I'm done!

Freya Hardman (9)
Hoe Bridge School, Woking

Growing Up

Growing up is super tough,
At some points, it feels very rough,
I want to play on the computer all day,
But of course, Mother says, "No way!"
What? Huh, homework?!
No, Mother, I'm not doing any of it today,
What's the point of it anyway?

I think she's being a bossy bee,
Wouldn't it be fun if I were her and she were me?
Though I'd have to keep her safe and sound,
And also look after her health all round!
It would be nice though, to have *someone* to boss around.
I'd let her eat sweets all day,
And never say no to anything she says.

But on the flip side, you see,
Being an adult is as hard as can be!
Mopping the floor, dusting the door,
What else is there to bore?!
Way too many chores!
Now I understand, you can't have a perfect life being a child or a grown-up,
I think I'd rather be... a pup!

Annika Sharma (9)
Hoe Bridge School, Woking

All He Wants Is To Defeat His Opponents

My tennis racquet always seeks out the ball,
Somehow pulling my body along to the call,
But if it misses, it sometimes gets frustrated,
Smashing his head on the floor.

It seeks out the positioning of the ball,
Its nose locking onto it.
Before he hits the ball, he circles to gain momentum,
Then he tenses, ready for the impact,
And sends it straight back to the opponent.

Like a zebra, it has black and white stripes,
As fierce and ferocious as can be.
The grip - so perfect for his master holding it,
They merge and melt into each other,
Agreeing - but also alien - he shouts as he hits the ball.
But his companion dampener is on his torso,
Reminding his strings to stay quiet.

Unfortunately, he has to let go of some of his strings,
They are too old to help.
When this happens, he has to go to the doctor.
It is painful, he is left with a bare frame,

But it is worth it.
He smashes the ball, perfectly in the middle,
His trustworthy friend at his side.

All he wants is to defeat his opponents,
If not, he stays calm, and thanks them for the game.
If put into the wrong hands, he fails,
There is no bond between him and this imposter.

At some point in his life, he would like to travel the world,
As there are many amazing racquets he can meet.
For now, the feel of the heat releases him.
Blazing bright and igniting the soul,
A fierce delight to unlock the truth in his life.
And on we go - battling again and again.

Gregory Avent (11)
Hoe Bridge School, Woking

The Runaway Rascal

A s anger brewed in the castle,

N othing stirred but a runaway rascal.

G rowing quickly day by day, he was fixed on flesh and food he found, tearing and scaring the others.

E xploring the unexplained, what he found was an unfortunate flying lemur.

R ecently, the clever little lemur had gotten trapped, but he knew he had to escape, so he had already pre-made a plan with his brothers.

E bullient, the tiger pounced towards the lemur, but the clever little lemur had revved his engine... *Vroom! Vroom-vroom!*

D esiring a snack, the tiger ran after him, eyes pierced, target locked. It led him back to where his heart lay, at the castle with Papa Lion and Mama Tiger.

J ade, lush leaves hung on every tree,

O rbiting the jungle like a bee.

"Y ahoo!" yelled the lemur, whizzing by - he had outsmarted the tempered tiger!

F lying up and beyond, near the glistening, eerie midnight moon,

U nfortunately, his engine failed... *Puff, puff, clank, clank!*

L evitating was no option, but falling was.

L achrymose thoughts filled his mind, so he sadly glided to the ground.

"Y ikes!" he yelled. He held a power coupling: three, two, one, *neyow!* His engine re-engaged. Not only was he joyous, but he was flying once more.

F rom up and down, from anger to joy,

U nite and be friends, no matter what.

N ever again did the tiger run away, nor did the lemur fly.

Arthur Ramsey (10)
Hoe Bridge School, Woking

Spiron

Treen trees towering, gigantic creatures roam,
Occasloudly letting out a giant groan,
And in the *cepths* of the forest roams Spiron,
With the body of a lion and teeth of iron.

Trees *hiver* as this creature comes by,
Or when it lets out its *hollowing* cry,
And then at *fiast*,
A child comes past;

And in his hand,
Was a *magicerous* flask,
Containing some *sheadly* sand,
Which could wipe out an entire land.

The flask *ripened*, and the Spiron's *slimusting* head,
Detached from its body, it lay dead.
Planquil and peaceful, the forest was left alone,
Now the Spiron was eventually gone.

Once, *treen* trees *stowered*, *gigary* creatures roamed,
Occasloudly letting out a giant groan,
And in the *cepths* of the forest roamed Spiron,
With the body of a lion and teeth of iron.

Key
Treen: tall and green
Occasloudly: occasionally and loudly
Cepths: centre and depths
Hiver: hide and shiver
Hollowing: howling and bellowing
Fiast: finally and last
Magicerous: magical and dangerous
Sheadly: sharp and deadly
Ripened: ripped and opened
Slimusting: slimy and disgusting
Planquil: placid and tranquil
Stowered: stared and towered
Gigary: gigantic and scary.

Daniel Whittaker (11)
Hoe Bridge School, Woking

The Gimbleweeblysheevly

Linner had just arrived, and the shmungus
Was gricking to the sun,
As bink trees rested on the gair
Oh, how the trif sun shun.

As the impresting barnings
Scathered through the land.
"Beware of the Gimbleweeblysheevly!
And beware of its pricking hand!"

Looking in the Gincle Gree
You could see the one beast.
With its slimpy skin and its gracoflaps,
But the best was its spinkly eyes looking at its feast.

On thy eyes the Gimbleweeblysheevly
Had wacleins, and on its big head
It had a flacap, but what was unbelievable
Was its fiwat-proof skin.

Stretching over to the Blumpy Tree
Its long neck scraped past the branches
Skimming them to their very greb.
It was flobbling over to the wanches,
But a devastating occurrence stopped it.

Its tutu got stuck!

You could hear it cry for hours as it tried to unjangle,
But it was so trapped in the bush it couldn't let free.
Its words of sorrow cried over the land as it untangled,
So sad that it had to let the tutu be.

As it disappeared back into the Gincle Gree you could just see.
A sharp thing poking out, it was its lashing scistal.
Looking out to the shore, you could see more in the sea,
All slaphing in the waves, as they disappeared.

Eleni Kavakiotis (11)
Hoe Bridge School, Woking

The Trap

In the corner of the forbidden room,
A place with a dusty old broom,
There is a monster by the name of 'the Trap',
That is ravenous and kills with a *snap!*

This was the story Sam was told,
But now, as he was old,
He went to his dad,
Who said that he wasn't an old enough lad.

But as the boy walked back,
He started to pack,
A sword, a bow,
That could pack a blow.

But could it hurt the terrifying Trap,
Who would probably have a painful attack?
Facing a monster with such tremendous power,
It would be difficult with no place to cower.

He carefully walked to the room,
Under the silhouette of the ghostly moon.
The door behind him closed on its own,
He started to stop feeling the comfort of his home.

Tip, tap... Tip, tap...
Tip, tap... Tip, tap...
He heard a snap,
Was it the Trap?

And suddenly, *it* came out,
A monster with a long snout.
With sharp claws that sting,
And huge, long wings.

The boy struck it hard with his bow,
The monster cowered after the blow.
The boy, with one more strike, slew the beast;
And now, he was going to have a big feast.

But was the beast *really* dead?

Vahin Akkari (10)
Hoe Bridge School, Woking

The Monster Under My Bed

It was dreadful every night,
Every night, I would get a fright,
Waking up and turning on my bed light,
My dreams swiftly flying away like a kite,
As I worried that the monster would bite,
Some time through the night.

One night, I'd had enough,
I knew that the monster was tough,
I knew that I didn't have much stuff,
So, as I picked my weapons up, I was worried,
Worried that I might not have much luck,
Clearing the stuff under my cramped bed,
Thoughts were droning on in my head.

Finally, I saw the monster,
The monster under my bed,
As soon as my weapons sped,
Sped round the monster's head,
The monster's face turned blood red,
And the monster was soon dead,
"I have slain the prey," I said.

It was dreadful every night,
Every night, I would get a fright,

Waking up and turning on my light.
But now I knew that I could sleep tight,
All through the night,
With me flying in my dreams like a kite,
To new destinations with pretty sight,
With the pride of a warrior, I said to myself,
"Goodnight."

Shivanjali Kanwar Narban (11)
Hoe Bridge School, Woking

My Headmistress Is A Lump Of Cheese

My headmistress is a lump of cheese
Please believe me, oh please, oh please
I told you my school is a bit crazy
No, I'm not a daisy

Oh, did I mention my form teacher
Is a big slice of mozzarella pizza?
I told you my school is insane
And no, I'm not a plane

Although my art teacher is
Once she jets away, it leaves a tremendous fizz
The rest of us just stand around
Making no sort of sound

My DT teacher is a saw
We couldn't ask for anymore

So as you can see, my school is good in some ways and
bad in others
Oh, I forgot to tell you about my brothers!

They don't go to my school,
Apparently, theirs is super cool!

Now my hand is super sore,
But maybe I should tell you some more.

My swimming teacher is floaty,
And everyone is super GOATy (Greatest Of All Time, at
swimming, obviously),
My English teacher is like a book,
And everyone has to look,
For her amongst her bookcase.

I told you my school was mad,
No, I'm not a notepad!
So now you can see, my school...
Is super cool!

Clemmie Lees (9)
Hoe Bridge School, Woking

The Graposerpent

Shistening in the moonlight,
Shimmering so bright,
The forest lay
In the middle of the night.

"The Graposerpent, my dear,
Is a creature to fear,
Head of a ricious dog,
It reeches at passers-by
Just like a frog and a fly."

And just like that, the boy had an idea.
He would rid them of all the fear.

He had been waiting for this kind of opportunity,
To be a famous part of his community.
So he finished the beast in one big *slash!*
And for celebration, one big *bash!*

When he got home, he told the nory,
And then he felt a rush of glory.
He had rid them of this ugly beast,
And would now have a feast.

Shistening in the moonlight,
Shimmering so bright,

The forest lay,
In the middle of the night.

Glossary
'Shistening': shining and glistening
'Ricious': ravenous and vicious
'Reeches': roars and screeches
'Nory': news and story.

Freddy Aldridge (11)
Hoe Bridge School, Woking

The Graposerpent

The sky was grey.
The planets were a glushy green.
The grass was as dry as hay.
Night in the forest was silent.

The Graposerpent glided down the dirt path.
Hoofing anything in its way.
Now, if you were to face its wrath.
Never look at those beady eyes.

On this night he was slithering extremely fast.
Everything just flew past.
Without warning, he halted, only to find a man.
Holding an elegant sword.

The Graposerpent looked at him and the man looked
back.
The Graposerpent's eyes had a different beam in them.
They were pleading, he was sorry for his misbehaving
and ready to be slaughtered.
But the man accepted his apology and dropped his
precious sword.

He would not kill this animal.
All living beings deserve a second chance.

So, he left the Graposerpent in peace and visited him once in a while.
But, one day, he never came back. I wonder why.

Arjan Jutla (11)
Hoe Bridge School, Woking

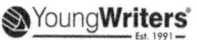

A Blank Canvas

My paintbrush sweeps along the canvas
Swishing and swooshing with glee
Gliding across with no sadness
Dancing and prancing went he,
It possesses my hand
Like a scavenging creature
It creates nothing - nothing bland
In a coat with a button to feature,
Crimson - amber and russet;
Olive - pear and mint;
Azure - sapphire - violet;
Silver - dusky and flint.
It gargles and sips,
It drinks and it swills,
By watercolours it tips
Its slender bill,
It surfaces from the disc of paint,
It peers out the window at landscapes and trees,
What should it do - the paintbrush so great?
Should it paint forests, skies or seas?
It thinks and it thinks - sniffling and snuffling,

It stares at the canvas, thinks of the great,
It rearranges its fibres - rifling and ruffling
And continues, continues to paint...

Emilia Reynolds (11)
Hoe Bridge School, Woking

I Dream

I dream of Winter Wonderlands,
A walk with you and me.
Of beaches with bright, golden sands,
Looking 'pon the deep, blue sea.

I dream of towering mountains,
Reaching for the sky.
I dream of icy glaciers,
A sparkle in my eye.

The dream flies back, the dream unwinds.
Reality, with sharpness, finds,
The quiet space where I recline.
Then back I drift with a relaxed mind.

Beneath the sky, so bright, the sun.
The day begins, the world is fun.
It rises high, the race begun.
We run through fields, our souls as one.

The morning's gold, not one to shun.
The warmth it brings for everyone.
A new day's here, the work is done.
And love arrives when sets the sun.

Matthew Janson (10)
Hoe Bridge School, Woking

The Danger Of The Quill

My quill swept along the page
Dressed in a feathery plume
Like a lady at a ball
Dancing the night away.

It wrote only to bring crime and sorrow
I looked on as it formed ink into words
Grudgingly quenching its thirst when required
Drowning pages in its work.

I dropped into my chair at dusk
The feather held in a jar
Twitching furiously
Still throbbing with life.

As it dragged my hand along pages
I thought wistfully of buns and tea
While it scratched away feverishly
Sniffing out titbits of sentences.

But I just wish for an easy life
And as I lay my quill down
As I collect up the pages of my work
I realise that you never get one.

Amelie Flude (10)
Hoe Bridge School, Woking

The Sights That Hurt My Eyes

The sight that hurts my eyes,
Are just a bunch of flies!
They dance and twirl,
Sometimes they even go into a swirl!
The sight that hurts my eyes is chilli powder,
When you blow it, the screaming gets louder!
The sight that hurts my eyes,
Is when my corgi has a boogie!
The sight that hurts my eyes,
Is when the phone pays its loan!
The sight that hurts my eyes,
Is when the butterflies sit on my nose and disturb my snooze!
The sight that hurts my eyes,
Is when the pilot goes to the toilet!
The sight that hurts my eyes,
Is when a train goes down a giant drain!
The sight that hurts my eyes,
Is when the bee stings me!
What are the sights that hurt your eyes?

Shraddha Varambally (7)
Hoe Bridge School, Woking

The Animal Orchestra

The lion roars a mighty tune,
His voice as loud as the silver moon.
The monkeys chatter, clap, and play,
Drumming leaves in a swinging way.

The dolphins leap, they splash and spin,
Their laughter bubbles deep within.
The owls hoot in the midnight air,
Soft as whispers everywhere.

The wolf howls long, the crickets sing,
The fireflies dance with glowing wings.
The buzzing bees hum low and sweet,
A golden song in fields of wheat.

From jungle deep to ocean blue,
The animals play a song so true.
A world of music, wild and free
Their voices make a melody!

Henry Damen-Turner (8)
Hoe Bridge School, Woking

The Night

The night,
Nocturnal birds have flight
And the trolls fight
A horrible fight,
All night.

The hard dark night,
Bare, bitter, and it will bite.

The sky so black like coal
And a big black hole in my heart.

The hard dark night,
Bare, bitter, and it will bite.

The moon, so bright
It gives a luminous light,
Beaming from the rocky orb.

The hard dark night,
Bare, bitter, and it will bite.

Black silhouettes tower over me
As I lose my power so slowly.

The hard dark night,
Bare, bitter, and it will bite.

Despite the cold dark night,
I shall stay to fight
For what is right.

Harriet Hellings (9)
Hoe Bridge School, Woking

The Tiger

Tiger Wyger, don't be shy,
Otherwise, you're gonna cry,
After that then you might get yourself into a fight.
If you fall then we'll call, call, call!
The hospital.
When you're ready go to that,
Go to that odd, odd lad.
Oh no! Tiger, you fell in pain,
Oh no, Tiger! Not again,
Maybe you should try to train, train, train, train!
Train until weak fades away.
Now that you've trained and trained,
Now you have to get that pain.
Scratch! Scratch! You got him! Yay!
Now what have you learned today?
Practice makes *purrfect!*

Alya Kumar (9)
Hoe Bridge School, Woking

Dragon Friend

P urple species that lived long ago.

U nder the caves where nobody goes is where they always go for adventures and fun.

R avenous creature that lives with might and always eats rocks without a blight.

G reat big dragon that lives in a house, on a mountain and on a couch.

O mnivore he is and likes to eat rocks so that's why he has four stomachs, and has no socks.

N aughty like others, but not like me. Also, he likes to go roly-polying just like me!

He rescues people and people ride on him as the clue.

Answer: Purgon.

Avinesh Ramanathan (9)
Hoe Bridge School, Woking

Hoffle And The Boffle

Once in the Tulgey Wood,
There was a boy who was very good.
Once this German boy named Hoffle,
Went out to kill the Boffle.
The Boffle likes to waffle, although it is a beast,
That really, really likes to feast.
The boy took his spear and threw it high in the air,
Which then pierced The Boffle's protective hair.
This caused the Boffle to die
And Hoffle said, "Bye-bye."
So the Tulgey Wood lived happily ever after with a
young king by the name of Hoffle,
Who famously killed The Boffle.

Sebastian Woodall (10)
Hoe Bridge School, Woking

The Dive

I see the water glistening
Before my eyes,
The sun is on my shoulders,
The board creaks beneath my toes.

I stretch my lungs full of air,
My arms above my head,
Flex my knees.

Fly through the air,
Arc in the sky,
Then

Blue.
Blue.
Blue.
Cold blue stream.

Arms are windmills powering me,
Legs are engines pushing me,
And my head is clean and empty.

Cold blue stream.

Wilfred Gagen (7)
Hoe Bridge School, Woking

My FavouriteToy

I have a favourite toy.
I've decided he's a boy.
He's called My Rainbow Bear.
I treat him well, with good care.

He likes reds, greens and purples.
His eyes are bright circles.
He has a loom band collar;
He wears it with great honour.

I've lost him hundreds of times
But he's back as midnight chimes.
He fills me with so much glee
And he means the world to me.

Maisie Reid (9)
Hoe Bridge School, Woking

Pyraminx

As
I was
Entering the
Room, my hands
Automatically pulled
Out my Pyraminx, and
I took my spot, looked at
My opponents and waited.
The Pyraminx started to swivel in
Front of my eyes, and I took my time to
Look at the other players. The Pyraminx also
Swivelled back and forth, as if looking at the other
Pyraminxes, observing the colours, until it lay solved.

Edward Barrett (11)
Hoe Bridge School, Woking

The Striple

Just a normal night, he thought,
In Jipsy Forest, oh how he fought,
Both weren't meek, rather quite strong,
And when he hit the Striple on the head, it went *bang*!
Oh, how he swung his blade,
Yes, the Striple was slain!
Then he galloped home,
All the way to the dome,
Kneeling at his master's knees,
He was given a lifetime supply of peas!

Nate Ferrier (11)
Hoe Bridge School, Woking

A Strict Teacher

I have a strict teacher,
She always hit you with a cane,
When you turn up late or you miss the train.

I have a strict teacher,
She always groans,
When you use your phone in her class or even at home.

I have a strict teacher,
She always gives you a detention,
For no apparent reason!

Menaal Reza (8)
Hoe Bridge School, Woking

The Homeless Man

I lost my house, my wife, my kid,
I remember when life was so sweet,
I started living on the street,
Drugs were taking over me.

I was left a lonely man,
Stuck in an endless time lapse,
Everything collapsed,
And toppled over me.

Without everything,
Without everything.

Harry Green (10)
Hoe Bridge School, Woking

An Unexpected Visit

The sky lights up, much to humanity's dismay,
Nothing will come out of it, the people pray.
Unfortunately, the universe is not always on their side,
When he appears, they better hide.

He has found their solar system and is looking for their planet.

They gather food in case of an emergency,
They enforce their rules of safety with urgency.
They make machines that slash the stars' energy,
His power can force them into extreme jeopardy.

The immense sun starts to flare,
A looming dread starts to fill the not-so-fresh air.
They are thinking about saying their last goodbyes,
They underestimate the power of their nasty surprise.

He has found their village and is looking for their bunker.

The ground trembles with unimaginable fright,
They do not know that above them is a beastly sight.
The wind starts to howl with fear,
Warning them that the creature is near.

He has found their bunker. Run.

Josiah Orji (11)
Lower Halstow School, Lower Halstow

The Homeless Fox

The snake slithered, slid to his house. Then he saw a fox hiding.
"Little fox, little fox, what are you doing?"
The fox said nothing.
"Little fox, little fox, could you leave?"
"No!" said the fox.
"Why?"
"Because my house got raided."

"Little fox, little fox, that is no reason to take my home."
"Hmm, no."
"Please?"
"No!"
"But why won't you leave?"
"Because if I do, I won't have anywhere to go."

The snake tried everything. He tried to give him pigeon, fish and rabbit, but then he thought of something.
"Little fox, little fox, would you leave if I built you a house?"
"Yes!"

The snake slithered away and got started building a home. He spent a day and a night, and finally...

"Little fox, little fox, I finished building!"
The little fox ran out of the house and to his new one.
Then the fox ran and gave the snake a hug.
"Thank you!"

Arthur Dowdell (11)

Lower Halstow School, Lower Halstow

Waiting, Waiting, Waiting

Riding on the violet winding road,
Looking at the peasant toads,
His greed is a wild animal,
Even sometimes acting like a cannibal.

Tap, tap on the old indoor,
Impatiently waiting like a boar,
He whistled a graceful tune,
Out came a beautiful lady with eyes as bright as the
moon.

I will come at dawn tomorrow with a surprise,
It will be expensive buys,
Clip clop, the Highwayman trotted by,
Bess let out a heartfelt sigh.

Staring at the bright blue moon,
Waiting for his romantic tune,
Not knowing Tim the Ostler is near,
Soon the soldiers will appear.

Knock, knock, soldiers waiting at the door,
Bess' life will be no more,
Fingers are tied and bound,
When will her love be found?

Gun pointing at her breast,
Hoping for a long long rest,
Getting ready to prepare,
Taking her last breath of air,
Boom!
The trigger was shot.

Cleo Cairns (11)
Lower Halstow School, Lower Halstow

Germans Vs British

A military tank pulled in,
As something happened to the Germans' skin,
Then one German pulled out an RPG and shot,
Now, there was no tank. They had to do something,
and that was plot.

Five of the British got rifles and peeked over the trench
walls,
One of the British shot a German in the head, and he
falls,
The Germans then knew what they had to do,
They couldn't afford to lose any more of their crew.

Then, without warning, there was a cawing from above,
Then they all realised it was a dove,
All of a sudden, about five aircraft soared over the
British to attack,
That's when the Germans' sight went cold, empty and
black.

The British climbed over the trenches to attack any last
survivors,
They agreed to set traps, starting lots of fires,
And they thought they would win,
And they did, and celebrated with many full bean tins.

Edward Jessey (11)
Lower Halstow School, Lower Halstow

Seasons

There are four seasons,
But you don't know the reason,
One is hot, one is cold,
One is when leaves fall from the trees that are gold.

The first season is spring,
This is when all the birds sing,
Happy lambs are jumping around,
The lambs are white and brown.

Secondly, it's summer,
But when it comes to an end you become glummer,
The days get longer,
And the nights get shorter.

All of a sudden, it's autumn time,
And the leaves start to climb,
The temperatures drop,
And the days stop.

Finally, winter's here,
Which means Christmas is near,
It's always windy and wet,
But it's not summer yet.

Evie Nije (10)
Lower Halstow School, Lower Halstow

The Super Squad

Saving people,
Saving cats,
Saving flats from giant hats.

The Super Squad is here,
And hear the people cheer!
Their fabulous future awaits,
And they also train with weights.

They attack villains with care,
Including Mr and Mrs Hair.
There is Mr Big
And his wife who likes to dig.

The Super Squad is here,
And hear the people cheer!
Their fabulous future awaits,
And they also train with weights.

Miss Thunder, Mr Lightning are a rightful pair,
Mr Wash has underwear for hair,
And his wife sits on a chair
And the vicar reads a prayer.

The Super Squad is here,
And hear the people cheer!

Their fabulous future awaits,
And they also train with weights.

Henry Williams (10)
Lower Halstow School, Lower Halstow

Death

You feel your fingers start to shrink
Then you feel like you can't blink
You look around and see the sky
Then you see angels float by

You see a man
Standing with his clan
Then you realise you're on clouds
But the man says you're not allowed

So you fall and see red
And there are people that are dead
Until you find yourself on ground
And you start to look around

You realise you're in the pits of hell
And more people fell
Then your head starts to spin
Then you see your heart in a tin
Then you take your last breath
And then wonder, is this my death?

Kian Godden (10)
Lower Halstow School, Lower Halstow

Death

You could hear fingers falling apart
And all the cracking.
You could see bones poking out of skin
All you could see were bones.
Breath screeching from the door behind the graves
I've had a war but I died.
I feel like this because I have fallen off a cliff but
All my bones fell out.
All I saw was the moon with a devil's face on it
Scratching forks all over the wall.
Shouting everywhere
From all the dead people.
In the morning, the sky is red
There's fire everywhere.
I keep burning my feet...

Lara Pina (11)
Lower Halstow School, Lower Halstow

Moon

The moon glimmered,
Lighting up the forest.
But a passing cloud covered the moon.
The trees, in a panic,
Put their branches in the air
Like they just don't care.

Josephine Shilling (10)
Lower Halstow School, Lower Halstow

There's A Monster On My Lunch Tray

There's a monster on my lunch tray,
It's munching on my cheese!
It slurps up all my yoghurt,
And makes a monstrous sneeze.
It's swallowed up my baguette and burped out loud for fun!
And now it's licking up pudding pots - someone call my mum!

My teacher says, "Don't be absurd! Monsters don't eat ham!"
But when she turns her back, I see it nibbling at my jam.
It waves at me, winks at me, and does a monster jig!
Then vanishes in the dustbin, with a dance that's rather big!

The Magenta Class
Lycée International de Londres Winston Churchill, Wembley

Seasons Of The Year

Different seasons, differences for you, for us,
You are beautiful,
I am grateful,
Summer is hot,
Autumn is not,
Winter is cold,
Spring is gold,
Summer, spring, autumn, and winter,
The seasons of the year.

Seasons,
Of,
The,
Year!

Different seasons, differences for you,
For us.
You are beautiful,
I am grateful,
Summer is hot,
Autumn is not,
Winter is cold,
Spring is gold.
Summer,

Spring,
Autumn and winter,
Are the seasons of the year!

Yazid Choulli (8)
Lycée International de Londres Winston Churchill, Wembley

Cat And Bat

Cat sat with Bat on the mat. Cat wanted to go play with Rat, but Bat wanted to sit down with Cat.
Cat said, "I declare a paddle battle with rattles in Seattle."
So, as she said, they did. Once they were done, Cat won because she stepped on Bat's shoes.
"Woo, woo!" Cat said while taking Bat's shoes! But Cat and Bat forgot the fight, so they could play with Rat and sit on the mat.

Marlie Germain (7)

Lycée International de Londres Winston Churchill, Wembley

A Little Dinosaur

There once was a dinosaur who was lonely and sad.
Along came another dinosaur, they put snails on their
nails. The spiky dinosaur shared his pillow, their names
were Spiky and Dindy.
"Is it a berry? Is it a house? It is very big, is it a bear?
It's a bear!"
They ran into the woods, terrified.
"It is scary," said Dindy.
"It is dark," said Spiky.

Marina Baldini (8)
Lycée International de Londres Winston Churchill, Wembley

Love

A little hug gives lots of love to everyone.
A little love from everyone is up and down but never stops.
No littering, no pitying just so much love and fun.
I think it's over me.
People dancing in the streets,
The music is echoing through their feet.
Birds are singing,
Oh, the daylight is so bright.

Chloé Shahbahrami
Lycée International de Londres Winston Churchill, Wembley

Friends Forever

F riends forever
R acing down the hill
I n the park having fun
E njoying their time together
N ever giving up
D ancing in circles
S inging as loud as they can
H iding behind trees
I n the park, having fun
P laying forever.

Isabella Laborieux (7)
Lycée International de Londres Winston Churchill, Wembley

Space Planets

Planet limes are all green,
But the universe, bubblegum.
It is multicoloured and brittle,
Dotty, oh how little it is!
The Milky Way shines as bright as a diamond.
But planet holes are so deep.
Nobody ever explored them.
Then there is the planet Star,
I don't know where you are.

Georgia Le Junter-Sleath (8)
Lycée International de Londres Winston Churchill, Wembley

Childhood

C hildhood is a big memory,

H ighs and lows,

I n your life,

L ive through success,

D ull mistakes to learn from,

H ide your mistakes,

O r just carry on,

O h, you can never read the world,

D ig deep to succeed.

Kaimu Brugger (8)
Lycée International de Londres Winston Churchill, Wembley

Spring Is Here

F irst the flower sprouts.
L eaves turn bright green and gleam in the sun.
O rchids rise from the ground.
W illow trees start to grow higher.
E vergreen, evergreen, don't be mean.
R oses smell stronger, so that means spring is here!

Ava Daniel (8)

Lycée International de Londres Winston Churchill, Wembley

The War Of 1509

The war was dangerous, violent, and cruel.
The war for England really was.
Thousands died and who won?
The underrated Saxons, of course!
King Alfred, the hero of all.
It was brutal, bloody and bad.
The war of 1509 really was.

Venkat Sundaram Lee (9)
Lycée International de Londres Winston Churchill, Wembley

Seasons

S eeing the birds fly in the sky
E ating under the sunshine
A rainbow lighting across the
S ky
O ther tree apples grown
N ear the river, drinking champagne
S pring is coming soon.

Zoé Adjido (7)

Lycée International de Londres Winston Churchill, Wembley

Fluffy, Fluffy

Fluffy, fluffy kangaroos are puffy
Fluffy, fluffy bunnies go *boingy*
Fluffy, fluffy pandas go buffy
So fluffy, fluffy kangaroos are puffy
Fluffy, fluffy bunnies go *boingy*
Fluffy, fluffy pandas go buffy.

Aline Bachir (7)
Lycée International de Londres Winston Churchill, Wembley

Mother Nature

Oh Mother Nature, oh Mother Nature
You give us flowers
You give us fruits
Oh Mother Nature, you are so good
You give us water, you give us air
You give us everything to live...
... And enjoy.

Neil Gala (7)
Lycée International de Londres Winston Churchill, Wembley

The Dangerous Cyber Planet

The dangerous cyber planet
Is a planet where everything is possible.
But you just need to be careful
Because when the pipes burst
A giant storm comes
And the planet gets sucked in.

Noah Lepelletier (7)
Lycée International de Londres Winston Churchill, Wembley

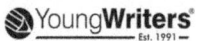
Dogs

A dog is fluffy,
And cute and furry and strong
And good at walking.
And likes nature,
Dogs have puffy cheeks and diamond eyes.

Jasper Josias (7)
Lycée International de Londres Winston Churchill, Wembley

Snake Halloween

S nakes slither soundlessly.

N aughty snakes bite carelessly.

A ll kinds of snakes are venomous.

K iller snakes are not nice.

E vil snakes are mean like Lightning McQueen.

H alloween is spooky, it sends shivers down your spine. Obey the rules

A nd only take one piece at a time.

L ollipops, Haribo, Sour Patch Kids and more.

L eprechauns, witches, robots and more.

O ne wrong move and you're gone forever, the witches' curse will make you shiver.

W hining in pain as wolves rip apart your body.

E ating sweets after all those scares.

E erie bats flap around, soon you'll be sleeping soundly.

N ow there's no need to scream, the jack-o'-lantern's coming for me! Argh!

Archie Winnett (11)

Marshwood CE Primary School, Marshwood

Autumn Woods

A clear, crisp breeze sweeps through the wood,
Sending a carpet of leaves dancing.
A fox stalks in its bright red hood,
Its little white socks prancing.
The leaves change quickly from fresh greens to warm
browns,
Soon to fall to the wet, moist ground.
As the days get shorter, the moon comes out,
Yawning as it illuminates the nocturnal creatures'
nights.

The old oaks whisper secrets along the gentle breeze,
Animals busy gathering food for winter's freeze.
As an owl soars across the milky sky,
A buzzard swoops and lets out a ghostly cry.

Tabby Travill (9)
Marshwood CE Primary School, Marshwood

Halloween

H alloween is when people get pumpkins and carve them.

A fter that, they put them on their dangerous doorsteps.

L arking around with haunted houses and ghosts.

L ess and less trick or treats by the day.

O ver the day, getting more and more sweets.

W icked witches having fun in the moonlight.

E nd of all the treats, but it's nice to keep treats.

E ver seen a ghost? Well, they are scary.

N ever ever go out on Halloween night.

Rosie Knight (8)
Marshwood CE Primary School, Marshwood

Autumn Leaves

A ll the leaves are reddening in a bunch,
U nder the oak trees,
T he leaves go crunch,
U p in the air, a cool, chilly breeze,
M any trees lose their leaves,
N othing says that they all do though.

L ucious times have gone,
E ven though some are still green,
A t the summer, the sun shone,
V erses now, it is nowhere to be seen,
E lves start to come,
S ave yourself something for Halloween.

Kiki Crane (10)
Marshwood CE Primary School, Marshwood

Halloween

H alloween is a grateful time of the year,

A ll the people gather to trick or treat,

L et yourself be yourself,

L ight your lamps like animals' eyes glow in the dark,

O h, you must thank people who treat or trick,

W olves howl loud,

E vil pumpkins show teeth,

E very Halloween ghosts rob,

N ever fear! Put some sweets in the box.

Grace Johnson (8)
Marshwood CE Primary School, Marshwood

Halloween

H aunted
A mazing
L oved
L aughable
O ptimistic
W onderful
E pic
E njoyed
N ighttime!

I ndependent
S uper!

T ense-free
H elpful
E xotic!

B rilliant
E scaped spirits
S tupendous
T reat haul!

Louisa Grinter (9)
Marshwood CE Primary School, Marshwood

Rainforest Pain

The rainforest is still and quiet,
Where the red-eyed tree frog lives.
With the toucan birds and chimpanzees,
The sloths are moving slowly through the green bushy trees.
If you stand still and listen,
You will hear the hummingbirds singing a soft little tune,
And raindrops dripping from tree to tree.
We need to save our rainforests.

Edith Hooper (10)
Marshwood CE Primary School, Marshwood

Halloween

Halloween, pumpkins orange,
Black and yellow, faces carved,
Trick-or-treaters at the ready,
Witches ready, goblins googly,
Spirits of brides,
Bony, bony, spooky-dooky,
Treats for trick-or-treaters
Bony, bony, spooky-dooky Halloween
Spooky-dooky Halloween
I shall be the ghost queen.

Ivy Partridge (7)
Marshwood CE Primary School, Marshwood

Goodbye Winter Nights, Hello Summer Days!

Spring. My favourite season,
Shall I tell you the reason?
My birthday's in it, that's the reason!
New beginnings, coming alive.
Cold, clean, crisp air
Spring's seed appears from thin air.
Goodbye nights of winter's gloom
Hello, days of summer's bloom.

Humphrey Leeds (8)
Marshwood CE Primary School, Marshwood

My Lambs

C ute
H yper
U nique
R oguish
C harming
H appy
Y outhful

A ctive
N ippy
D elightful

T iring
Y ielder
S oft
O utdoors
N ice.

Erin Churchill (10)
Marshwood CE Primary School, Marshwood

Falcon's Feelings

F alcons fly free

A bove the tall trees

L et go of the horrible feelings

C uddle with calm nature

O pen your massive heart to brilliant meanings

N ow leave sadness for another time later.

Elsie Ballam (11)
Marshwood CE Primary School, Marshwood

Giraffe

G entle, calm giant
I nfinite spots
R eaching tall
A cross the trees
F inding leaves
F leeting noises in the breeze
E normous neck stretching far.

Charlie Battershell (9)

Marshwood CE Primary School, Marshwood

Nonsense Cat Comedy

There was a cat that sat on a mat
That was big and fat
Like a hippopotamus
That had learnt how to meow
Whilst lying in a canal.

Albert Brum (7)
Marshwood CE Primary School, Marshwood

January Is...

January is a rope, pulling me into the new year,
January is a train, and the next stop is adventure.

February is a bridge, bringing people together,
February is a park, now the year is in full swing.

March is a wave, washing away my winter worries,
March is a door, opening into the blossom and rain.

April is laughter, jokes and joy,
April is the sun, warming my heart.

May is an artist, bringing colour to the leaves,
May is a path, leading to a tropical jungle.

June is the warmth on the back of my neck,
June is the sun, bringing smiles to our faces.

July is shells washing up on the shore, bringing hope
and joy,
July is a palm tree, sheltering us from the heat.

August is the sun setting for the end of summer,
August is the sand between my toes, relaxing me in
stressed times.

September is a school bell ringing,
September is the leaves falling.

October is a ghost, scaring us all,
October is the darkness, as the days get shorter.

November is a hand, picking the leaves off the trees,
November is a clock, ticking away till Christmas.

December is festivities and smiles,
December is a mirror, reflecting the year's good times.

Bea Godfree (10)
Pinewood School, Bourton

The Cruel Mosquito

There once was a cat called Cosi,
Who liked to chase big mozzies,
She chased them all day,
She thought it was play,
But then the mozzie bit Cosi.

There once was a cat called Cosi,
Who liked to chase big mozzies,
But then she was bitten,
As well as her kitten,
And that's how the mozzie bit Cosi.

There once was a kitten called Orca,
Who kind of liked to eat pork(a),
She, a poor little kitten,
By a mozzie, was bitten,
And that's how the mozzie bit Orca.

There once was a kitten called Orca,
Who was feeling a bit like a dork(a),
She, a poor little kitten,
By a mozzie, was bitten,
And that's how the mozzie bit Orca.

There once was a dog named Luna,
Who liked to howl at the moon(a),
She thought she saw a mosquito,
She remembered swatting it though,
But then she heard, "Time for food, Luna!"

There once was a mozzie called Mark,
The last thing he heard was a bark,
Oh, how he was swatted,
And his body it rotted,
When it went dark for Mark.

Wilf Llewellyn (10)
Pinewood School, Bourton

Normandy Landings

The sea was spitting at the boat
Hitting it.
Retreating.
But always coming back

Splash, splash...

People vomiting as we arrived
At the French border of Normandy

Bleurgh!

Clutching my pistol hard,
Germans opened fire.

Ratatata.

Suddenly the ship was covered by blood
There was a mad scramble.
Then I leapt into the sea

Shooting down like a missile

Down, down.

There was a moment of silence
To think about
What had just happened.

I broke the surface and
The cold hit me like a fist.
Gasping air.

Aaaaaahl

People
And
Corpses
Dropped down
One
By
One

Splash by splash.

I got a mouthful of saltwater
As people died around me.

Died.

To shore I came
Firing every step.

Ratatata.

Arlo Dawson
Pinewood School, Bourton

Weather

The wind is my brother slapping me in the face
The wind is a wolf howling in the moonlight
The wind is a playful puppy chasing its tail around and
around
The wind is a train taking me on different adventures
The sun is an emoji smiling down on us
The sun is my friend, shining bright, always there to say
hello
The sun is an alarm clock waking me up to start a new
day
The sun is a buttercup blooming in the meadow
The rain is the tears of a baby giant
The rain is a waterfall washing away my picnic
The rain is a maze of mirrors as the puddles get bigger
and bigger
The rain is a refreshing drink on a summer holiday
The snow is Jack Frost leaping across the garden
The snow is a lion biting off fingers
The snow is a dream, waking up to find yourself in a
winter wonderland
The snow is an icicle hanging down until one day, the
sun will come out and everything will just melt away,
like a snowman on a hot, hot day.

Roxie Spooner
Pinewood School, Bourton

The Final

I walked out onto the pitch, which was a roaring storm
of fans
The match kicked off, and I sprinted as fast as a rocket
To tackle the boy with the ball, with a crash, bang and
wallop
We rucked like strong, muscly rhinos
We broke their defence like a rock crashing through
the surface of the sapphire water
We passed, and the ball flew like a graceful eagle
I dived and scored like the sun rising over a
gargantuan mountain
When we won, the stadium erupted into a rainbow of
different emotions
When we lifted the trophy, we were like a happy,
overjoyed family
The final was over!

On the rugby pitch
I tackled, tackled like a knife through butter
I rucked, rucked as strong as a rhino
I broke the line like a plane tearing through the sky
I ran, ran as fast as time
I scored, scored like an overjoyed bumblebee
We won, won like proud lions.

Guy Ashcroft (9)
Pinewood School, Bourton

Emotions

I'm circling
I'm twirling
I'm about to start hurling

I'm shaking
My brain breaking
I'm trying to start making an idea of what's going on

My brain's dying
I'm about to start crying
I'm still trying to keep hold
But I'm not too bold

I'm shivering
Always quivering
Everyone tries to make me wither

I feel like I'm getting killed
I feel like I'm getting bullied
But I wish I could get drilled instead

It's all emotions
It's all nothing but commotions

I'm trying to reach an answer

Like in maths I always say I can't sir, but in my brain
There's a storm with lots of rain

But I'm going to sleep
Away from the dark deep
By day there are monsters and ogres but by night
There can be flight.

Ivo Eddell (9)
Pinewood School, Bourton

Six Nations

S izzling in excitement, the English and Welsh fans gathered at the front of the stadium, waiting for the game.

I ncredible tries were scored every minute by England. The fans were so excited for the final results of the match.

X mas is over, now it is time for the rugby season to start.

N one of the English fans were thinking that we would lose.

A mazing songs were played in Twickenham Stadium.

T alented players were running around the pitch trying to get a try to win the match for the team.

I went to the match and it was phenomenal in the stadium. The songs were booming out of the speakers all around me.

O ver the try line England kept pushing and pushing and pushing until they got a try.

N one of the England or Wales players got injured in the match.

S uch a good score was made, England won 35-0.

William Newham (9)
Pinewood School, Bourton

166

Football

F riends and family love this game. Having fun and showing skills are the aim.

O ver the years, I love it even more. My happiness grows, especially when I score.

O h, this sport brings me so much joy! Been playing this since I was a little boy.

T ension and drama are a part of it. As well as flashy shoes and a colourful kit.

B eckham, Ronaldo, and Messi are some of the greats. They gave it all, they went for it, whatever it takes.

A little boy like me can dare to dream. Hoping that someday I will play for the national team.

L ittle by little, day by day. Hard work and perseverance will get me there one day.

L et's not forget, before this poem is up. That I want England to win the World Cup!

Augusto Aquitania (9)
Pinewood School, Bourton

The Best Save Of All Time

Today, on a warm summer's night,
There is a football match.
The biggest football match of the century:
Little Rumbling Tummies versus The Gosberry
Snozberries.

On a pitch as green as mould,
The Gosberry Snozberries' goalkeeper
Is as short as an ant,
Waiting, chilling, dreaming.

But - suddenly! He hears a noise.
The Little Rumbling Tummies are running up the pitch,
He doesn't know what to do!

Something squirms and squiggles in his tummy,
It's as if he's going to burst!
Instinct takes over.

He does a cartwheel -
An amazing, magnificent cartwheel.
He glides through the air.

The ball stops dead
Right between his legs,
He is an upside-down hero!

The crowd goes wild
It is the most magnificent
Save
Of
All
Time!

Louis Leach (9)
Pinewood School, Bourton

Winter Is Coming

Snow is coming
Children are playing in the snow
It's all *crunch, crunch, crunch*
The grass is crispy and cold
The trees sparkle in the sun

Children are making snowmen
Snowball fights are on
The cold breeze is biting everyone's faces as it dances
along
A warm fire is on in each and every house

Hedgehogs are getting ready
Hiding underground
Snuggling up with one another
Their long spines prickling everyone

The dormouse is also there
Under the frozen ground
Hiding from its protector
And getting frost all over its hands

It's the end of winter now
Spring is here, flowers up
Colours are smudging everywhere

The animals are up
Leaping in the warm spring air.

Amelia Goodhew (9)
Pinewood School, Bourton

War

I see the men lining up for the war.
I hear airship sirens from miles away,
The noise is like an earthquake,
I see mothers waving their children goodbye at the station,
Hugging their loved ones goodbye,
Promising to write.
Women are left in charge,
Maybe they will get to vote?

Crash, bang, the bombs are falling.
The Nazis have arrived.
The war has come,
The war has come,
Hide in your homes,
Run away.
Guns cracking,
The war has arrived.

The men are coming home,
The war has ended,
The Nazis have fled.
I hear the women crying,
Their loved ones never returning.

The battlefields are covered in mud.
But one tiny red flower appears.

Davina Woolley (9)

Pinewood School, Bourton

Chaotic Wind

The weather is a key, unlocking a cage
Suddenly, people get knocked off their feet
Something is gnawing at the leaves on all the trees
Suddenly, something is howling out of nowhere...
It's havoc
There are weather warnings north and south
There are stormy seas east and west
Everywhere, stuff is flying -
Bins
Roof tiles
Leaves
All of it is flying
It's like a plane is carrying it
Suddenly, everything falls
It gets warmer
Weather warnings go away
Seas turn into flat sapphires
That means the wind is gone
Hooray!
But be warned, it will come back...
Maybe like a hurricane
Or a light breeze
All I know is, it will come back.

Alistair Wilson (10)
Pinewood School, Bourton

Pinewood School

P eople playing in the sun,
I nclusive fun for everyone.
N eeding a friend is important in school,
E ven if you think you're too cool!
W alking alone can be dull and boring,
O penly wishing you were playing football, scoring.
O h, please ask me to play, you think in your head,
D reading the bell with your maths lesson ahead.

S houting comes from across the field,
C ome watch this; it's Manchester vs Sheffield!
H ysterics and laughter everywhere,
O ver here and over there.
O n the fields, the children play,
L ook around; it's another beautiful day.

Maya Lewis (10)
Pinewood School, Bourton

Outer Space

Outer space is a wonderland full of stars and planets
Outer space is a star that you can wish on
Outer space is a spark of hope for a new species
Outer space is a home for planets and stars
Outer space is a Milky Way waiting to be explored
Outer space is a black hole engulfing everything in its way
Outer space is a forest for stars
Outer space is a mystery waiting to be uncovered

Outer space is so big and bright
Show me your inner light
Over the moon and in the stars
Maybe you'll find Mars

Maybe this is a new life
Or maybe you'll find a wife
Oh space, oh space, so big and bright
Show me your inner light.

Elise Campbell (11)
Pinewood School, Bourton

History

"H errerasaurus!" the rhino shouted as it ran rapidly through his hole to find meat to have, meanwhile, its three-metre-long body smashed into stuff.

I n medieval times, menacing men malleted innocent men, but nowadays we just use guns and bombs.

S ometimes, I see Roman soldiers fighting Britannia brutally, but only in my dreams.

T he Egyptians worshipped crazy gods like Ra, the god of the sun.

O h wow! Joe Biden loves his big bag of bourbons buried in Biscoff.

R omans raided rich villages ravenously around the raiding years of 50 BC.

Y aks are what Egyptians used to transport food, valuables and even people.

Monty Dearden (10)
Pinewood School, Bourton

History

H arold Godwinson. Don't take any ideas from him! He can't control countries for a living.

I nvasion of the Romans. Deadly, deadly! Don't mess around. You'll just hear a *bang! Crash!* And a *whallop!*

S panish Armada. It was the best weather England got all year.

T -rexes don't like being woken up because they are always dino-snoring.

O h, wow! The Romans really rudely invaded Britannia.

R eally rapid racers ring rudely at the doorbell like deadly hippos.

Y ou know the punishments back in the old days were exceptionally brutal and fierce like Harald Hardrada.

Xander Clarke (10)

Pinewood School, Bourton

Iron Man Is...

Iron Man is a lightning, crashing thunderbolt going 100 miles an hour.
Iron Man is a bulky, strong, hard rock.
Iron Man is an alert, angry cat.
Iron Man is a big, dangerous stallion.
Iron Man is a multi-transforming human with branches.

Iron Man is always on it.
When someone's in trouble he'll be there to save the day.
Iron Man saves the good from the bad.
Iron Man is an athletic person training for the Olympics.

Iron Man is able to fight as many people as he wants at once.
Iron Man is as powerful as Godzilla.
Iron Man is a beast.
The whole world at once couldn't take him down.

Dhruv Chukka (10)
Pinewood School, Bourton

A Poem To The Flowers

F lowers, you bring joy to everyone that sees you, like a rainbow in the sky of a heavy storm

L and would love to be covered by you, with your greens and blues as you dance across the fields, gobbling them up

O pen air would suffer if you were not there, blooming big everywhere

W ith your vibrant colours everywhere, people can't be happier

E veryone can see your beauty from miles away, like the prettiest girl in the world

R ed, green, blue, orange are your colours, most vibrant in May when the rain has gone away

S uper songs are made about you because you are bright, brilliant every day!

Esme Erskine Crum (10)
Pinewood School, Bourton

The Clock Inside A Wall

There once was a house with a clock inside a wall,
No one really liked it, it disturbed one and all.
Each day the sound would put people astray,
It was relentless, like the sun on a hot summer's day.
So they listened closely to find from where it came,
When the right wall was found, then began the game.
Of smashing and bashing as hard as they could,
Until the wall no longer stood.
When the dust and debris had finally stopped,
Their gaze fell upon that annoying, ticking clock.
They cracked it and crushed it into tiny little shards,
Ah! Silence!
Now they could hear the wind whistle through the
yard.

Sebastian Dobney (9)
Pinewood School, Bourton

Space Is A Library

Space is a library:

Shelves of mystery waiting to be discovered and read
Silence creeps up all around - shh...

Mars, the action section - fiery explosions, heart racing
I keep searching for the next big thing

Earth arrives - science, nature and geography
Mountains stretch to the sky
Oceans digging deeper than the edge of space

Stars in the sky, endless possibilities
Like words on a page

And finally, Pluto - cold and fantastic
Like Narnia

Space is a library
Shelves of mystery waiting to be discovered and read
Silence creeps up all around - shh...

William Mackay (11)
Pinewood School, Bourton

I Love Summer!

Summer comes every year
Summer comes with a fresh glass of beer
Summer comes with a snap of a finger
Summer comes and smells of flowers linger

Summer is my dry, hot hair dryer
Summer is the splashing sea dripping in faster
Summer is like a volcano spilling out lava
Summer comes around just like karma

When summer comes to an end
These wonderful memories bend
The diamonds in the galaxy slowly freeze
Making a cold, nasty breeze
When the diamonds start to drip
Summer will give you a warm sip
Even though spring is so great
Summer is next!
I just can't wait!

Francesca Walker (10)
Pinewood School, Bourton

Imagine

Imagine we are on a black horse
Clippety, clippety, clop, we leap in the field
The air is fresh and clear.

Imagine we are in a field, we smell the smell
Of soft wet moss
We hear the *crunch* of leaves as we
Trot along.

Imagine we are in a forest
Filled with adventures to seek and
Stories to tell.

Imagine we are soaring in the air
Over crumbly bridges to leap, and fields
For plants to grow and grow. Imagine
We soar over a forest full of exciting
Stories to tell. Imagine it,
Just you and I in a
Place where you could be anything.

Mary Ingham (10)
Pinewood School, Bourton

The Seasons

Spring is like a first step,
Spring is a first step,
Spring is the start of the beginning
And the end of the start.

Summer is like the first hope,
Summer is the first hope,
Summer is the first hope
And the bearer of fun and sun.

Autumn is like a snake shedding its skin,
Autumn is a snake shedding its skin,
Autumn is a snake shedding its skin
And a wave of colour.

Winter is like a blanket being pulled over the sun,
Winter is a blanket being pulled over the sun,
Winter is a blanket being pulled over the sun
And a darkness that seems eternal.

Arthur Ferguson (11)
Pinewood School, Bourton

Mockingjay

The Mockingjay unfurled its wings
Its mighty, mighty wings
And sang a song, a beautiful, bold song
The verses that fluttered out of the bird's mouth
Were a mellifluous harmony,
Dazzling passersby.

Sitting on a windowsill
Chirping among the trees
Everyone went quiet, even the bees
Those Mockingjays in the trees.

Red plumes, fire burning and raging
Flowed to their necks and down, down, down, down
Past their tail feathers so if they flew by
All you saw was fire 'catching fire'
Like a flaw
Those Mockingjays in the trees.

Archie Colquhoun (11)
Pinewood School, Bourton

Three Meals Of The Day

Scrumptious and delicious
Sleepily, hungrily, quickly, I demolished the sizzling
bacon
Scoffing, munching and chomping the scrambled egg
on my plate.

Lunch
Yummy and big
Angrily and furiously, I chomped and chomped
Until not even a crumb was left.
Chomping and crunching on my chips as they
disappeared one by one.

Supper
Squishy and slimy
Tired and lazily, I chewed on my broccoli as it mushed
in my mouth.
Mushing and munching, I gobbled down the last of my
supper
Until there was nothing left
Except for the *broccoli!*

Max Heaton (10)
Pinewood School, Bourton

The Lost City

Green, dripping, lush
Trees like towering skyscrapers

Dark, damp, humid
The forest floor is decaying

Squawk, rustle, roar
It's like the jungle is talking

Silent, gentle, slow
A sloth moves past

Stumble, trip, crack
Dead twigs cry out

Grinding, winding, falling
Vines wrap and dangle from the sky

Aching, sweaty, exhausted
My legs fall to the ground

But then, in the distance
It's emerging from the mist

The lost city appears
Relieved, elated, done.

Max Tilney (10)
Pinewood School, Bourton

Love

What is love?

Love is a warm hug on a winter's night,
Pulling you in and holding you tight.

Love is a cat, purring, nestled in your lap
Or softly mewing at a nearby bat.

Love is a friend, helping you out,
Wiping your tears, making sure you don't pout.

Love is nature, all around,
Making the calmest rustling sounds.

Love is family at Christmastime,
Toasting the season with a warm mince pie.

What do you love?
Have a long think because it's a big question.

Rosie Lawless (11)
Pinewood School, Bourton

Summer

Summer is a time for laughing and having fun
Playing and swaying in the brightly burning sun
Is where I belong
If you feel sad, summer is always there for you
With amazing ideas
And a million happy thoughts
All you need to do is step outside
To feel the warmth

Summer is a time for looking up high above
Seeing clouds changing shape
Like shape-shifters
In the sky
While you're drinking cold summer drinks
With umbrellas for shade
Nothing more is needed for a perfect summertime.

Florrie Horton (9)
Pinewood School, Bourton

My Rabbit Ate My Mum's Purse

She's not going to be happy,
She said this could be the actual worst,
If something touched my new purse,
Oh, no! This is bad, this is horrible,
We're going to get in lots of trouble,
Dad said, "We need to be fast, we need to be quick,
otherwise Mum will think this is all a trick!"

My rabbit ate my mum's purse,
We need a plan, we can buy another,
Or get it from that man,
He won't gnaw or chew this one, we are sure,
But now we need to get it from the bottom floor.

Imogen Workman (11)
Pinewood School, Bourton

Summer Days

Oh, how I long for summer days
When the trees are bright
Oh, what a lovely sight
When the birds come out from sleep.

Oh, how I long for summer days
Where we wear skirts and tops every day
These days are so crisp and coarse.

Oh, how I long for summer days
Where the horses play
Under the shining sun.

Oh, how I long for summer days
When animals come out for a peep
And flowers come out from sleep
Spring, summer, autumn, winter
Such a long time to wait!

Lily Lewis (10)
Pinewood School, Bourton

Playing Cards

P laying cards with groups of friends
L earning rules - the fun never ends
A ctions depict cat or mouse
Y elling yippee when you win
I ntricate cheaters missing a go, suddenly beaten by marvelous Mo
N ecessary numbers, marching in line
G reat for socialising

C lubs as black as night
A ces winning, high or low?
R ummy, reciting numbers and suits
D iamonds dance and twinkle red
S olitary solitaire.

Joe Rajapaksha
Pinewood School, Bourton

The Different Seasons

Autumn brings beautifully coloured leaves lying
Motionless on the hard, frozen ground
Autumn is when all the poor animals have to hibernate

Winter is like a barrier holding back the sun
Winter is a barrier holding back the sun
Winter is when we all stay at home by the warm,
soothing fire

Spring brings happiness and fun to all of us
As we are all really looking forward to the wonderful
summer sun
Spring is the new upbringing of all the beautiful
blossoming flowers.

Freddie Campbell (11)
Pinewood School, Bourton

Six Nations

Six Nations is a time to spend with family
Six Nations is when a ball gets powerfully kicked
Six Nations is an egg-shaped ball that is thrown around
Six Nations is when players get tackled and crushed
Six Nations is so teams can tackle, kick, and pass.

Dupont is a quick, fast, intelligent player
Dupont is a quick rugby player who never misses a crunching tackle
Dupont is a quick trophy-lifter and a grand slam winner
Dupont is a brisk passer, passing as far as the stars.

Reggie Parsons (11)
Pinewood School, Bourton

I Know I Saw A Monster Underneath My Bed

I know I saw a monster
I don't know what to do
Should I tell my friends
Or even call the zoo?

I know there is a monster
Underneath my bed
His tongue is spotty yellow
And his eyes are fiery red.

I feel there is a monster
Something tickled my toes
I laughed so much
I went the colour of ruby rose.

I believe there is a monster
He made a terrifying roar
It was like a ferocious bear
I can't bear it any more.

Martha Hyde-Smith (11)
Pinewood School, Bourton

The Wonderful Life Of A Frog

In a quiet pond, under the moon's glow,
Frogs in green cloaks hop to and fro.
With a leap and a splash, they sing through the night,
Croaking their tunes under starlight so bright.

Bright eyes gleam, their chorus fills the air,
A melody of nature, sweet and fair.
From leafy pads to the pond's cool edge,
They perform nightly on the water's ledge.

So when frogs croak as the cold night darkens,
It's their little Coldplay concert.

Ruan Moelwyn-Hughes (11)
Pinewood School, Bourton

My Dog

Loving, kind, and gentle,
Wouldn't hurt a soul.
If you made him mad, then he'd
Scratch your soul.

We go to the park,
I chase him everywhere.
He chases other dogs,
Who knows why?

We go to the butcher, he jumps
At all of the beef.
I call him 'bad dog'.
He still gets a treat.

His favourite time of day is supper,
Can't help giving him beef.
He leaps up to my bed and
Curls up with me.

George Wynn-Williams (9)
Pinewood School, Bourton

Space Friends

Two girls, a boy and a dog went to space
In a beautiful tube rocket dressed in lace
They saw five planets and went to the fifth covered in
gold
They went up to two aliens being very bold
The aliens turned out to be very kind
They were called Lily and Max and had big minds

Night after night, they dined on the moon
Holding a great big spoon
They loved it so much, they decided to stay
Olivia and Max fell in love and got married straight
away.

Valentina Kidson-Trigg (10)
Pinewood School, Bourton

Seasons

Leaves glowing
Daffodils opening
Trees growing
Flowers unfolding
What more could you wish for

Sun beaming down
On the leaning town
It is so bright
It looks so white
I feel so alive

The crunchy orange leaves change colours
From orange to yellow to brown
The branches are left with no leaves

As cold as ice
Covering up to your knees
Just like a blanket
Then crunching through the snow.

James Hosken
Pinewood School, Bourton

The Seasons

Winter is the start of a new year
Winter is the beginning of a different race
Winter is a sheet of ice covering the warmth of the sun

Spring is the start of a new beginning
Spring is when the sun and flowers open up
Spring is the time when the blossom starts blooming

Summer is the time when the heat burns your skin
Summer is when the seaside is your friend
Summer is a wave of holiday taking you away to
scorching islands.

Bella Russell (10)
Pinewood School, Bourton

Nature

N ature is all around us, up down, round and round,

A nimals prancing and dancing and having fun,

T rees swishing and swaying in the cool afternoon breeze,

U nderneath the tall, towering oak trees, hidden in the shade, is where tiny tortoises lie,

R ain... pitter-pattering on the top of the canopy, trickling down the tree trunk,

E nd of the poem, I have to leave, the sun's going down at a frightening speed.

Annie Sharman (10)
Pinewood School, Bourton

Skating

S kating is a place I can be me and I can set my world free.

K icking low in to my spin, turning and turning, never giving in.

A n imaginative roller coaster through my life.

T rying to keep up on the work I have to do.

I n my world that blade is my brain.

N othing is easy, you just try your best.

G oing to competitions is sometimes hard but with my skates in my hand, I will keep going far.

Beattie Simons (9)
Pinewood School, Bourton

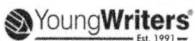
Rex The Spaniel

Rex the spaniel, the colour of honey
His nose as brown as chocolate
His collar, the colour of a red poppy in a French field

Rex the spaniel, barking at my feet
Begging, begging to go for a walk
Looking up with his wide eyes drawing me in

He chases his tail round and round
'Til he falls to the ground
His shaggy coat in waves of colour
Glistening in the French field
That is my spaniel, Rex.

Aluna Angus (10)
Pinewood School, Bourton

Pink Is...

Pink is my favourite colour.
Pink is the magical streaks in the twilight sky.
Pink is a blooming flower.
Pink is a playful pig.
Pink is the neon pop on the perfect rainbow.
Pink is the crazy colour of love.
Pink is a delicate, soft heart.
Pink is fluffy frosting on my favourite French Fancy cake.
Pink is a fuchsia flamingo balancing on one leg.
Pink is my favourite pose and colouring joy into every empty space.

Rose Bartlam (9)
Pinewood School, Bourton

Dragons

Once, there was a time when dragons ruled land, sea
and sky
Destroying all enemies that tried to come by.

Sea serpents, ice wings, exterminators, land wars, all
were easy to find
But rarest of all was the dragon king. Bones of his
enemies, he would grind.

Ripping, biting, hunting as they came
If they did not kill, they would maim,

Tearing down armies to claim
The dragon age came.

Theia Grewal (9)
Pinewood School, Bourton

Outer Space

The sun is a big ball of fire and
It gives light to the other planets.

Astronauts fly off from Earth
To the dusty old moon.
When they land, they float,
Like the sea and a boat.

The asteroids bomb down to Earth
At lightning speed,
Like 40,000 miles per hour.
A ball of rock that's on fire,
So big that it goes faster and faster,
Hurtling through the sky.

Petra Durrant (9)
Pinewood School, Bourton

Kindness Is...

Kindness is a warm, snuggly teddy bear in a cosy, sleepy bed.

Kindness is a sapphire crystal glittering in the twilight sky.

Kindness is a graceful star dancing in the marshmallow clouds.

Kindness is a small child helping someone up.

Kindness is a magic wand that changes people's lives.

Kindness is a helping hand full of love and joy,

Kindness is the glue that keeps this world in one.

Alice Longe (10)
Pinewood School, Bourton

Winter

The cold wind told a story about snow and ice
That slithered up your back and trapped you in a vice.
It nipped at your toes like a tiger,
Follows dark shadows of any that oppose.
The frozen flowers are statues of ice,
Until the sun comes out and unleashes its powers.
The lakes start to melt,
The difference in climate can be felt,
Everything comes alive like a giant beehive.

Archie Giverin (11)
Pinewood School, Bourton

The Journey Of Life

A fresh start,
New to a journey called life.
A snake shedding its skin
Or a crab bursting out of its shell.
Into a whole world of secrets and lies,
Of friends and enemies.
Of life and death.
Life is a mountain to climb
And suddenly I am halfway up,
The cold ripping at my skin,
Begging me to slow down
But now I am in my stride
Nothing is slowing me down.

Wilfrid Bird (11)
Pinewood School, Bourton

Horse Riding Is...

Horse riding is a magical adventure through worlds with animals so enchanting and tame.
Horse riding is a world full of freedom and miraculous fun.
Horse riding is wild adventures over jumps and races.
Horse riding is a happy hobby where you build a connection with a horse.
Horse riding is an enthusiastic adventure through walking, trotting, cantering, jumping and galloping.

Georgia Finch
Pinewood School, Bourton

Space

What is 25,000 miles around the middle
But also six billion trillion metric tonnes
And able to float?
What homes eight billion people
And 196 countries
Where some live in harmony
And some in war
And some just live on the road?
The Eiffel Tower, the Statue of Liberty, Big Ben:
All landmarks

Am I this or that?
Take a guess...

Fenner Owen (11)
Pinewood School, Bourton

February Is...

February is a brick wall you must climb into spring.
February is depressing and grey, leaving behind the
jolly season.
February is a grey, cramped box to hold too few days.
February is a grey pavement that no one knows about.
February is an egg-shaped rugby ball being tossed
around by the Six Nations.
February is a swinging season between winter and
spring.

Quintus Vero (10)
Pinewood School, Bourton

Growing Up

When young, you play with toys,
When you grow up, you hate the noise.

When a teenager, you sleep more,
When older, you get a job. What a bore.

When you're older, you may get married,
And you never know, a child may be carried.

When you're older, your hair may go grey,
But if you're not careful, it may all go away.

Arthur Clark (10)
Pinewood School, Bourton

Nature

N ipping frost in the morning sun.

A pples ripe and juicy, falling off the ancient tree.

T ulips bursting boldly out of the ground in spring.

U p above me, sensational birds are soaring through the air.

R oses fill my glorious garden with the sweet smell of summer.

E arwigs clamber in the cracks of the uneven stones.

Harry John (9)
Pinewood School, Bourton

Jack Moss

J ack Moss is a lovely person.
A t break, he plays football.
C aring and sharing, a lovely man.
K ind and generous Jack Moss is.

M ost good-hearted person in the world.
O ptimistic he is, and very happy.
S uccessful at keeping friendships alive.
S porty and fair worker in a team.

Jack Woddy (9)
Pinewood School, Bourton

Six Nations

S uper speedy passes
I ncredibly awesome tries
X mas season over, rugby season on

N asty tackles
A chievements of a lifetime
T errific performances
I mpossible, unexpected victories
O pportunities for the underdogs
N ightmare kicks
S uper speedy passes.

Alex Tomanek (11)
Pinewood School, Bourton

Space

I went up as fast as lightning
I soared through the air
I saw the planet Quadruple
It shimmered and it shined

I soared and I soared
Just to find out
I was on the planet Quadruple!

I couldn't stay there
I took off again
I landed on Earth
Very blue, just to my liking
So I stayed!

Freddie Leggate (10)
Pinewood School, Bourton

Emotions

Anger is a wave of pain floating through your mind.
Fear is darkness spreading through your body.
Stress is your life wobbling.
Sadness is everything you own disappearing.
Envy is wanting more than you need.
Embarrassment is being abandoned.
Excitement is all you ever wanted.
Happiness is light guiding you.

Julius Steele (11)
Pinewood School, Bourton

Turtles

T iny tanks walking around
U sually, his walking has no bound
R ising out of the water for a breath
T anky turtles aren't afraid of their death
L azily swimming looking about
E ating algae and giving a shout
S wimming away from a shark's snout.

Oscar Subba (11)
Pinewood School, Bourton

The Cameraman

The cameraman
Stood in a campervan
Holding a rifle
Eating chocolate trifle

The enemy came
Lowering bombs from a crane
Holding swords
And wooden boards

Down came the planes
Sending water exploding from drains
The pilot eating cake
For a random sake.

Rory
Pinewood School, Bourton

Space

Space is cool, just like football.
It's big and it's dark,
It's wide and it's stark.

Space is black, you don't go back.
Space is scary, you must be wary.
Space is full of planets swarming like gannets.
Astronauts explore for a door to snore.

Ben Workman (9)
Pinewood School, Bourton

March Is...

March is an animal breaking free from its cage
March is a tiger pouncing on its helpless prey
March is a doorway out of a long, cold, dark tunnel
March is a flower ready for spring
March is a blank sheet that has been painted with
beautiful points of nature.

Ivo Robertson (10)
Pinewood School, Bourton

Space

S aturn burning bright in the dark, dark night
P lanets all around like lights shining bright
A steroid belt like a ribbon in the sky, small bits of rock flying high
C ould a fantasy be more real?
E pic facts about this thrill!

Adam Willis-Hill (11)
Pinewood School, Bourton

Nature

N ow stop and admire the stunning sunset,
A lways buzzing with insects galore.
T he most gracious friend I ever met,
U p above me, the cottony clouds soar.
R oaring rivers under towering trees,
E veryone, respect nature, please!

Harry Vane-Tempest (11)
Pinewood School, Bourton

Having Friends

Friendship is the warm feeling of being together,
Friendship is laughing with someone.
Friendship is playing and having fun.

Friends cheer you up when you are mad,
Friends do favours for you,
Friends help you get through hard times.

Charlie Gantlett (9)
Pinewood School, Bourton

226

Rugby Tackling

Rugby
Violent and vicious
Violently, quickly and briskly
Tackling, scoring, celebrating and kicking

Tackling
Aggressive and fierce
Viciously, fiercely and furiously
Crashing, crunching, obliterating and smashing.

Max Charlton (10)
Pinewood School, Bourton

Space

S olar systems whizzing round like a merry-go-round
P lanets discovered, new life found
A steroids destroying Earth
C an we discover more new birth?
E pic discoveries and more to come.

Duncan Ogilvy (10)
Pinewood School, Bourton

Space!

S un, stars, moons
P lanets make the universe lively
A steroids zooming past stardust
C enturies of spinning around black holes
E verything shines in the dark of space.

Jack Moss (10)
Pinewood School, Bourton

Friendship Is...

Friendship is kind and warm, like a blanket
Friendship is gentle, like a happy land.
Friendship is amazing and great.
Friendship makes you feel lush inside.
Friendship is all I could ever wish for.

Issy Lloyd (10)
Pinewood School, Bourton

Save Our Animals From Pollution

P ollution is bad for animals far and wide, enjoy this poem and read with pride

O rcas and fish are affected by pollution too, help them and they won't want you to shoo

L ilacs and other flowers find it hard to bloom under the silent boom of pollution ahead

L ittering is another form of pollution and is full of sin if someone doesn't throw something in the bin but instead on the floor

U nder us and above us, pollution is happening, stop the fuss.

T hanks and rewards are given to the person who will stop pollution. Even a gibbon could win

I n fact, littering could be done in a group, even by the rapper Snoop

O ily oceans gasping for breath

N ow is the time to help, don't be too late!

Tate Osborn (9)
Pix Brook Academy, Arlesey

The Aliens In Outer Space

A liens come to invade Earth in fleets of UFOs

S ometimes, they spy on us using their intergalactic telescopes

T he aliens also sometimes encounter NASA spaceships

R iots of aliens soon land on Earth, asking for Earth to be blown up

O ver 1,000 UFOs start to circle Earh

N ight begins as aliens land around Earth

A fter that, at sunrise, the skies darken as the mothership arrives

U SA military forces begin to attack with all their might

T he time has come for humans to become extinct, and aliens are victorious.

Rex Osborn (11)
Pix Brook Academy, Arlesey

Olympus

O lympian gods reside on the sacred mountain

L iving forever in the land of the immortals,

Y es, Mount Olympus is the home of the gods

M any gods live here, their power limitless,

P erhaps you do not believe me, but be warned, the gods may strike you down

U nless you make the proper sacrifices and honour their might,

S o the twelve Olympian gods, the cloud riders, the wave drivers, the Earth destroyers...

Ewan Ronayne (11)

Pix Brook Academy, Arlesey

Cute Animals

C ute animals everywhere
U s together forever
T o the moon and back
E at fruit with all your animals.

A s we get to the stars, we all fall asleep
N ever split up again
I n the stars I found you
M oon looking down on you, my friend
A ll I see is my cute animal
L et's see the galaxy
S oon I will be back to see my new friend.

Florence Harris (9)
Pix Brook Academy, Arlesey

Friendship

F riends in France eating fries

R ed roses in Rome

I gloos in ice

E milia is my best friend

N ever ending for forever

D ear friend on the pier

S hips on the harbour I see you

H i, oh no, bye

I miss you

P eering around then, now steering around.

Eden Chegwyn-Ross (9)

Pix Brook Academy, Arlesey

Heroes In Space

There was a hero but he lived in space. If there was an accident, he would save the astronauts and do anything to help them.

One day, a meteor was going to hit Earth. He needed to save the world. If he didn't, he would be no hero. His grip was too weak.

He pushed it away and everyone cheered and that was the hero in space.

Tyler Jones (11)
Pix Brook Academy, Arlesey

Felix The Fox

His name is Felix the Fox.
His fur so silky and red.
He has a big fluffy tail, and his personality,
So beautiful it has to be said.
He barks with loud enthusiasm.
He smiles with pure joy.
But with periods of busyness, he acts so very coy.
This is Felix the Fox, my beautiful boy.

Louisa Short (10)
Rose Lane Primary School, Romford

The Echoes Of Stone And Soul

Beneath the brittle bones of time,
Where winds wail with whispers of forgotten grime,
A fractured thought stirs, soft as the sinews of silk,
Woven with wonders, wound with wounds, waltzing
through milk.

Hark! The hollow hum of history's hand,
Trembles like thunder, twisted unplanned,
Yet in its endless echo, a story unsung,
A riddle that ripples, where the lost bells have rung.

In caverns of mind, where shadows once slept,
And histories heavy in silence have wept,
Friendship, like fire, flickers in frail fingers,

A flicker, a flame fragile yet fierce,
It rises, like rivers that roar and then pierce,
Through the fabric of night, through the fabric of grief,
A lantern that lanterns the soul's deep belief.

Mental mazes meander, muddled and marred,
With each twist a torment, each corner a scar,
But listen! The laughter of kindred hearts calls,
A chorus that clangs and a song that enthrals.

It's here, in the hum of our histories shared,
That wounds mend in whispers, where none are declared,
In the silence between moments, where shadows are cast,
Echoes of the past stretch but never quite last,
Like ink on old pages, their truth intertwines,
Threads of the present, pulling through time.

The past, like a phantom flickers and fades,
But its footprints persist in the paths that we've made,
In each heartbeat that echoes, in every breath caught,
We rewrite what history forgot.

The mind's mighty mountain, where madness may mount,
Yet friends find their footing in the slates that they count,
On the ledger of laughter, on the canvas of care,
A mosaic of moments, a mirror of prayer.

And in the end, as all riddles are solved,
The threads of connections in joy evolved,
Mental health is the mosaic, and friendships are key,
In the chambers of the soil, where we're all meant to be.

Noah Jolaoso (9)
Rose Lane Primary School, Romford

Friendship

My dear friends,
Who play football with me
And are kind,
Who play basketball with me
And are helpful.
My dear friends,
My dear friends.

Abdullah Ahmed (10)
Rose Lane Primary School, Romford

Spring Is My Favourite Season

Spring is my favourite season,
I love listening to the squeals of children playing outside,
Spring is my favourite season,
I hear birds tweeting and listen to what they are saying.

Spring is my favourite season,
I love feeling the warm breeze,
Spring is my favourite season,
All of the blossoms make me sneeze.

Spring is my favourite season,
I love the colour of the daffodils.
Spring is my favourite season,
Looking at all of the flowers on the windowsill.

Spring is my favourite season,
Listening to all the buzzing bees,
Spring is my favourite season,
Looking at all of the green leaves growing on the trees.

Jessica Waring (9)
Roseacres Primary School, Takeley

Mental Health

In recent times, there is a lot of serious concern,
All about one's mental health, there is so much to learn,
People suffer different things, they get worried and depressed,
They do not know what next to do and can become distressed.
If you see somebody struggling, please don't walk away,
If you just stop and talk, you may help them find their way.
They may need help that you can't give, but you can always ask,
There is such help available by those trained in this task.
Stop and listen to them, who knows, you may succeed,
To be the one who helps them to access the help they need.

Lacey Fuller (8)
Roseacres Primary School, Takeley

Out Of This World

In the sky way up high,
Many miles away,
We discovered many planets far, far away.

With Jupiter being the largest and Pluto being the
smallest,
We wonder what planet could be the hottest.

Now we know there are many planets near and far,
Sun, Mercury and Earth, including Venus
A shining star.

Now our journey has come to an end,
Let's discuss the planets,
Solar system and the Apollo 13,
Taking an astronaut, Neil Armstrong, to walk on the
moon,
Maybe we can continue exploring and will discover
more soon.

Sophia Taylor (9)
Roseacres Primary School, Takeley

Little Duck Learning To Fly

There was a little duck who couldn't fly
This made him very sad
All he wanted was to be up high
Flying along by his dad

"Flap your wings, son," Dad would say
"Give it another try!
Practice flapping all the day
And soon you'll be in the sky!"

Up and down his wings would go
Then suddenly, up he flew
"Look at me, Dad, I may be slow
But I'm now flying next to you!"

Jaxon Larman (8)
Roseacres Primary School, Takeley

All About Gryffi

My adorable dog Gryffi is very cute
He is always hungry but never for fruit
He cuddles me whenever I feel sad
He's very noisy but never bad.
He loves to be silly, getting dirty and wet
He will always fetch toys when I shout, "Get."
He is cheeky, chewing things he shouldn't
Like my shoes, I wish he wouldn't
I love my funny, furry friend
Because he is always with me, right to the end.

Ella Felton (8)
Roseacres Primary School, Takeley

The Jungle

In the jungle, there is lots to see
Snakes, monkeys and lots more to explore
Come down to the jungle and listen to the birds sing
And express their love to each other
Monkeys swinging on vines and playing hide-and-seek
Snakes rattling all the time
Be an explorer.

Thyri Cherrill (8)
Roseacres Primary School, Takeley

Friendship Story

One day, a girl went to school. She had no friends. Everyone looked at her. But a kind girl was there and wanted to help her. But the new girl ran away. Everyone laughed at the new girl. The new girl was crying until the kind girl came.

The new girl said, "If you came here to bully me, please leave me alone."

The kind girl said, "Just please tell me your name."

The new girl said her name was Sophia and the kind girl said that her name was Mary. Both of them started to become real friends. They stood up for each other. Sophia and Mary became friends and they were like true friends to each other. They lived like true friends after all they had been through, from bullying to best friends.

Khadija Bashir (7)
St Mary Magdalene And St Stephen's CE Primary School, London

My Trip To Lebanon

My trip to Lebanon was so much fun
I played in the water park under the hot sun
I went to the mountains that were so high
I met my cousins and ate some pie
My favourite activity was a zip line
I was so excited which was a great sign
I went bungee jumping, there was a nice view
I was high up in the sky that was so blue
I ate ice cream too, it was so sweet
I could definitely say it was an amazing treat
I hope I return and go on cool adventures
To make more memories and take incredible pictures.

Hamza Tabesh (7)
St Mary Magdalene And St Stephen's CE Primary School, London

The Unstoppable Cristiano Ronaldo

One day, the unstoppable Cristiano Ronaldo was born. The number 7 is famous, and so is his name, both coming along with his fame.

Starting with Lisbon, his favourite club as a kid, Cristiano was 12 years old when he began playing for Lisbon until a Manchester United scout noticed him and signed him. Ronaldo played for Manchester United for six to seven years. During his time at Manchester United, he was scouted again by one of the best clubs in the world, Real Madrid. Ronaldo rejected Real Madrid a few times but, suddenly, out of nowhere, he accepted the offer.

Cristiano flew to Madrid, which is in Spain. He arrived in Madrid to both love and hate. A few years later, Cristiano won his second Champions League and then three more with Real Madrid. He later moved to Italy after Real Madrid, then returned to England, where he played for Manchester United again but didn't really make history there.

However, he did make history in his career by winning five Ballon d'Ors, five Champions League titles, all the leagues he played in, and even more. He is simply the best player in the world.

Kyle Fleming (11)
St Timothy's Primary RC School, Glasgow

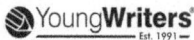
Bob's Bad Karaoke

There once was a man named Bob
Bob did karaoke for a job
He went up for a song and dance
Singing Lady Gaga's 'Bad Romance'
The crowd called a halt
And it was all poor Bob's fault
He was so bad at singing
Everyone's ears were ringing
People were filled with rage
When he went on the stage
A dark red tomato whizzed by his head
Everyone wanted him dead
Bob full of madness
Also a bit of sadness
Seas of boos
Which song shall he choose?

Jay Barwell (11)
St Timothy's Primary RC School, Glasgow

In Space

Stars and Mars
Go faster than history
The days passed like books past, each page
The space air is colder than an ice cream in a freezer
Wait, there goes the sunshine
The sky looking dreamier than a dream in bed
Galaxy glistening in the sky as bright as a moon in the
night
Stars dancing with joy
Black sky blacker than the black hole without the
yellow
That wishes the aliens to come to the Earth.

Radiant Lombardo (11)

St Timothy's Primary RC School, Glasgow

Shining Moon

Shining moon when it is night.
Shining bright.
The moonlight comes in my window.
One day I would like to go to the moon.
I open one eye, and I hear the moon quietly singing for me.
I would like to touch the shining moon.
How fantastic that would be!

Hana Zebri (10)
St Timothy's Primary RC School, Glasgow

Sting Of A Bee

With the look of a butterfly but the sting of a bee,
He would always say, "Security will never catch me."
He hates humans and mostly pets,
But when he is hurt, he has to go to the vet.
But he's just a normal butterfly with the sting of a bee.

Aarron Maley Turnbull (12)
St Timothy's Primary RC School, Glasgow

Through The Year

In winter, it's extremely cold
Warm hats, scarves and gloves are being sold
The glistening ice freezes on the ground
Even on a bird's nest, it can be found

In spring, colourful flowers bloom
The warm weather is coming soon
The fluffy lambs are being born
In cool ponds, frogs lay their frogspawn

The summer sun shines bright on me
On holiday, I feel so free
The ice creams are delicious and cold
"Put your hat on, Evie!" I'm constantly told

In autumn, the leaves fall
A hedgehog snuggles up into a ball
Dressed-up children trick or treat
Knocking doors for one last sweet

All four seasons over the year
Spending it with family I hold dear.

Evie Fallon (9)
Weddington Primary School, Nuneaton

Guess Which One

I rotate quite slow,
But there's something humans don't know.
I'm purely made of water and gas,
And how heavy I am in mass.
I'm extremely petite and round,
Nevertheless, I was the first planet to be found.
Unpleasantly, I smell like a rotten egg.
Me to the sun, I'm the size of a peg.
Not forgetting my ring of dust,
I really should clean myself, I must.
According to where I am in space,
Next to Neptune is my place.
You have done your job guessing about me,
Yes, it's Uranus, definitely.

Kenayah Kisempia (9)
Weddington Primary School, Nuneaton

Care Bears

Sunshine Bear loves to be bright,
When something's wrong, she helps with her light,
She floats onto the beach with care,
Hoping the sun will be in the air.

Cheer Bear loves to make happiness appear,
When something's wrong, she doesn't shed a tear,
She strides to the bed with care,
Hoping wonderful dreams will be there.

Grumpy Bear loves being grumpy,
He's starting to get a little lumpy,
He dawdles into the dining room, ruining fun,
And steals popcorn (a tonne)!

Amelie Thomas (8)
Weddington Primary School, Nuneaton

The Beautiful Game

Fans chanting in excitement.
People unite to cheer on their team.
The players are pumped and confident.
The opposition has a player who is very mean!

Sprinting for the ball that's in the air.
Fans are buzzing for a goal!
Referee makes sure the game is fair.
Players competing for their English soul.

Interviews take place after the game.
A manager will want to go home.
Only one squad will feel pure shame.
Whilst the winning team relax on their throne.

Theo Wright (8)
Weddington Primary School, Nuneaton

The Candy Land

I walked upon a forest,
And what in my wandering eyes should I see?
A magnificent, wonderful Candy Land,
Shining back at me.

Sticky toffee apples and liquorice leaves,
Hang from huge, chunky trees.
And away in the distance,
A scrumptious chocolate lake, if you please.

I picked up a bright pink lollipop,
Thinking it will taste of strawberries and cream,
But as I tried to lick it, I woke up,
It was all a dream.

Scarlett Pearce (8)
Weddington Primary School, Nuneaton

Winter

At wintertime,
All the birds chime,
And everyone stays joyful,
When everybody has family fun!

Everyone has great dreams,
As the Northern Lights beam.

On Christmas morning,
All the children are in surprise,
They all get their greatest prize!

As all the families are opening their presents,
Boom!
All the Christmas cheer,
Starts to appear!

Seth Thomas (9)
Weddington Primary School, Nuneaton

The Hero

A purple spark flickers in the distance and the hero
appears.
Dressed in black and white, the hero stands like a
statue, waiting for the right time to strike.
The hero possesses much power.
Calm and mysterious, the hero makes enemies shake in
fear.
As fast as lightning, the hero swoops and the enemies
are no more.
Who is this powerful being?
Who is the hero?

Olly King (8)
Weddington Primary School, Nuneaton

Football

F ans cheering, excitement all around,

O ffside, referee blows the whistle,

O h, no. Free-kick given,

T he crowd waits in anticipation,

B all is in the net,

A loud cheer fills the stadium, like a firework exploding,

L et's celebrate as they lift the trophy,

L ovely sight to see.

Edward Swift (9)

Weddington Primary School, Nuneaton

At The Seaside

A sunny day on the beach.
Scuttling crabs in cold, dark rockpools.
There's a happy, splashing child in the sea.
The water going up to his knee.

A clear blue sky with cotton wool clouds.
Surfers gliding on the waves.
A gigantic white seagull eating a chip.
Far on the horizon, I see a ship.

Jacob Wright (9)
Weddington Primary School, Nuneaton

Be Yourself

The best thing in the world is just to be yourself.
It does not matter what people think or say about you,
Just move on from that moment and enjoy the rest of the day.
Remember, tomorrow is a completely fresh day with new possibilities.
You can be whoever you want to be.
You just need to believe in yourself.

Oliwia Swietoslawska (9)
Weddington Primary School, Nuneaton

My Peaceful Place

My peaceful place,
Calm as it can be,
The sunset gleaming through the window,
Shining on my bed,
Birds tweeting fill the room,
Soon I fall asleep.

Chloe Ivers (8)
Weddington Primary School, Nuneaton

Am I A Monster?

I live in a forest,
I am long and thin,
I have a long tongue,
I can eat a lot of food.
Who am I?

Clayton Lai (9)
Weddington Primary School, Nuneaton

Moving Day

Sometimes all my feelings jumble around in my head like today, moving day. I took one last look at my room, one last glare out of the windows, one last turn of the doorknob. I stepped out of the room, turned my back to the door and burst into tears. I don't know why I did it because part of me was really excited to go and live with Grannie and Grandpa but it just felt better to cry. Mummy says that sometimes we need to express our feelings but they come out all wrong and that's just the way it is, but it doesn't make sense to me yet.

Seeing the house empty somehow made my heart feel weirdly cold and empty as the room itself. It was as if I had entered a whole new land. A land of nothing, no feelings, no object, no colour.

Downstairs was filled with boxes and up was another story, a very boring story. But only to the human eye was it boring, for hidden deep in the cracked paint on the walls were many happy memories. They were hidden in the small flecks of dust on the last unit. The hollow feeling in my heart still lingering, the soulful feeling hidden in the jagged slate on the roof, and right down to the familiar creak of the floorboards, it was all there...

Bonnie Withers (10)
West Wimbledon Primary School, Raynes Park

The Mysterious Wonders Of The Starry Archipelago

We invite you to this infinite space,
Glistening galaxies, moonlit Milky Way,
More mysterious miracles await.

Nebula after nebula, comet after comet,
Stardust after stardust,
Each constellation a story of inspiration.

As shooting stars whizz across Mars,
Whizz, fizz, whoosh!

Space is a boundless sea,
A mystery of gravity
That we can explore and see.

Shezmin Shameer (9)
West Wimbledon Primary School, Raynes Park

The Woods

There are footprints in the snow
Picked by the moonlight
Paths through the ancient trees
There they stop

Shadows twist up
Forming a cloud of darkness
A black shape
Shifting and shimmering
It hardens
Into a shard of black ice

Somewhere deep in the forest
Snow starts to fall
So
It
Begins.

Patrik Moise (10)
West Wimbledon Primary School, Raynes Park

Life

Life is good,
Life is bad,
Life is great,
Life is sad,
That's the world we live in.

We may just be children,
Children indeed,
But then we can plant the seed,
The seed that grows,
Grows more and more,
But we still don't know what it has in store,
That's the world we live in.

Madeline Moorfield (9)
West Wimbledon Primary School, Raynes Park

YOUNG WRITERS INFORMATION

We hope you have enjoyed reading this book – and that you will continue to in the coming years.

If you're the parent or family member of an enthusiastic poet or story writer, do visit our website **www.youngwriters.co.uk/subscribe** and sign up to receive news, competitions, writing challenges and tips, activities and much, much more! There's lots to keep budding writers motivated!

If you would like to order further copies of this book, or any of our other titles, then please give us a call or order via your online account.

Young Writers
Remus House
Coltsfoot Drive
Peterborough
PE2 9BF
(01733) 890066
info@youngwriters.co.uk

Join in the conversation!
Tips, news, giveaways and much more!

f YoungWritersUK **X** YoungWritersCW

◎ youngwriterscw **♪** youngwriterscw

Scan Me!